GREENS & GRAINS GOURMET

155 RECIPES TO NOURISH SOUL AND BODY

MATILDA L. SEEN

INDEX

Breakfast

Soups and Stews

Salads

Dinner

Desserts

Breakfast

Avocado Toast with Tomato

 1 serving 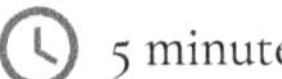 5 minutes

INGREDIENTS

- 2 slices of your favorite bread (sourdough, whole grain, etc.)
- 1 ripe avocado
- 1 small tomato, sliced
- Salt, to taste
- Pepper, to taste
- Red pepper flakes (optional)
- Fresh basil leaves (optional)
- Olive oil (optional, for drizzling)
- Lemon juice (optional, for a tangy flavor)

DIRECTIONS

1. **Toast the Bread:** Begin by toasting the bread slices to your preferred level of crispiness using a toaster or a skillet over medium heat.
2. **Prepare the Avocado:** While the bread is toasting, cut the avocado in half, remove the pit, and scoop the flesh into a bowl. Mash the avocado with a fork until it reaches your desired consistency. You can make it smooth or leave some chunks for texture. Season with salt, pepper, and lemon juice to taste.
3. **Assemble the Toast:** Spread the mashed avocado evenly over each slice of toasted bread. Top with sliced tomatoes, arranging them in a single layer or slightly overlapping.
4. **Add the Toppings:** For an extra flavor boost, sprinkle with red pepper flakes and add a few basil leaves for freshness. If desired, drizzle with a bit of olive oil for a rich finish.
5. **Season and Serve:** Give the assembled toast a final seasoning with a pinch of salt and pepper to taste. Serve immediately while the toast is still warm and crispy.

Vegan Banana Pancakes

 2 servings    15 minutes

INGREDIENTS

- 1 ripe banana, mashed
- 1 cup all-purpose flour (or whole wheat flour for a healthier option)
- 1 tablespoon sugar (you can use any kind of sugar, or substitute it with maple syrup)
- 1 tablespoon baking powder
- 1/4 teaspoon salt
- 1 cup almond milk (or any other plant-based milk of your choice)
- 2 tablespoons vegetable oil (or melted coconut oil), plus more for cooking
- 1 teaspoon vanilla extract
- Optional: vegan chocolate chips or blueberries for mixing into the batter

DIRECTIONS

1. **Prepare the Batter:** In a large bowl, combine the mashed banana, flour, sugar, baking powder, and salt. Mix well to combine. In a separate bowl, whisk together the almond milk, vegetable oil, and vanilla extract. Pour the wet ingredients into the dry ingredients and stir until just combined. Be careful not to overmix; a few lumps are okay. If you're adding chocolate chips or blueberries, gently fold them into the batter now.

2. **Heat the Pan:** Heat a non-stick pan or griddle over medium heat and brush with a little oil to prevent sticking. You can also use a cooking spray if you prefer.

3. **Cook the Pancakes:** Pour about 1/4 cup of batter for each pancake onto the heated pan. Cook until bubbles form on the surface of the pancake and the edges look set, about 2-3 minutes. Flip carefully with a spatula and cook for another 2 minutes, or until golden brown and cooked through. Repeat with the remaining batter, adding more oil to the pan as needed.

4. **Serve Warm:** Serve the pancakes warm with your favorite vegan toppings. Some delicious options include maple syrup, sliced bananas, fresh berries, vegan butter, or even a dollop of vegan yogurt.

Tofu Scramble with Spinach

 2-4 servings  15 minutes

INGREDIENTS

- 1 block (14 oz or 400 g) firm tofu, drained and pressed
- 2 tablespoons olive oil
- 1/2 medium onion, diced
- 2 cloves garlic, minced
- 1 cup fresh spinach, roughly chopped
- 1/4 teaspoon turmeric (for color)
- 1/2 teaspoon ground cumin
- Salt and pepper, to taste
- Nutritional yeast (optional, for a cheesy flavor), to taste
- 1 tablespoon soy sauce or tamari (for depth of flavor)
- 1/4 cup plant-based milk (optional, for creaminess)
- Fresh herbs like cilantro or parsley for garnish (optional)

DIRECTIONS

1. **Crumble the Tofu:** Start by crumbling the tofu with your hands or a fork into bite-sized pieces, mimicking the texture of scrambled eggs. Some people prefer smaller crumbles, while others like them a bit chunkier.
2. **Sauté the Onion and Garlic:** Heat the olive oil in a large skillet over medium heat. Add the diced onion and cook until soft and translucent, about 5 minutes. Add the minced garlic and sauté for another minute until fragrant.
3. **Cook the Tofu:** Add the crumbled tofu to the skillet. Sprinkle the turmeric and cumin over the tofu, and season with salt and pepper. Stir to combine everything evenly. The turmeric will give the tofu a vibrant, egg-like color. Cook for about 5-7 minutes, stirring occasionally, until the tofu is heated through and starts to get a little crispy on the edges.
4. **Add the Spinach:** Add the chopped spinach to the skillet, stirring until the spinach wilts and is well incorporated, about 2-3 minutes. If you're using plant-based milk, add it now to create a creamier texture.
5. **Season the Scramble:** Stir in the soy sauce or tamari and nutritional yeast (if using) for extra flavor. Adjust the salt and pepper to your taste.
6. **Serve:** Serve the tofu scramble hot, garnished with fresh herbs if desired. It pairs wonderfully with toast, avocado slices, or roasted tomatoes for a complete meal.

Vegan Blueberry Muffins

 12 muffins    35 minutes

INGREDIENTS

- 2 cups all-purpose flour
- 3/4 cup sugar (you can adjust according to taste or use an alternative like maple syrup)
- 1/2 teaspoon salt
- 1 tablespoon baking powder
- 1/2 cup unsweetened applesauce (acts as an egg substitute)
- 1 cup plant-based milk (almond, soy, oat, etc.)
- 1/3 cup vegetable oil (or melted coconut oil)
- 1 teaspoon vanilla extract
- 1 1/2 cups fresh or frozen blueberries (if using frozen, do not thaw)

DIRECTIONS

1. **Preheat the Oven:** Start by preheating your oven to 400°F (200°C). Line a muffin tin with paper liners or lightly grease it to prevent sticking.
2. **Mix Dry Ingredients:** In a large bowl, whisk together the flour, sugar, salt, and baking powder. This ensures that the baking powder is evenly distributed, which is crucial for a nice rise.
3. **Combine Wet Ingredients:** In another bowl, mix the unsweetened applesauce, plant-based milk, vegetable oil, and vanilla extract until well combined. The applesauce not only adds moisture but also binds the ingredients together, much like an egg would.
4. **Combine Wet and Dry Ingredients:** Pour the wet ingredients into the dry ingredients. Stir until just combined; it's important not to overmix to ensure the muffins stay fluffy. Some lumps are perfectly fine.
5. **Fold in the Blueberries:** Gently fold the blueberries into the batter. If you're using frozen blueberries, folding them in while still frozen helps prevent the batter from turning purple.
6. **Fill the Muffin Tin:** Divide the batter evenly among the muffin cups, filling each about 3/4 full. This allows room for the muffins to rise without spilling over.
7. **Bake:** Bake in the preheated oven for 20-25 minutes, or until the tops are golden and a toothpick inserted into the center of a muffin comes out clean.
8. **Cool:** Allow the muffins to cool in the pan for a few minutes before transferring them to a wire rack to cool completely.

Chia Seed Pudding with Mixed Berries

 2 servings  2 hours 10 minutes

INGREDIENTS

- 1/4 cup chia seeds
- 1 cup almond milk (or any plant-based milk of your choice)
- 1-2 tablespoons maple syrup or agave nectar (adjust to taste)
- 1/2 teaspoon vanilla extract
- A pinch of salt (optional)
- 1 cup mixed berries (fresh or frozen), such as strawberries, blueberries, raspberries, and blackberries
- Additional berries and mint leaves for garnish (optional)

DIRECTIONS

1. **Mix the Pudding:** In a bowl or mason jar, combine the chia seeds, almond milk, maple syrup (or agave), vanilla extract, and a pinch of salt. Stir well to ensure everything is thoroughly mixed. The chia seeds tend to settle at the bottom, so it's important to mix them properly.
2. **Let It Set:** Cover the bowl or jar and refrigerate for at least 2 hours, or overnight. This allows the chia seeds to absorb the liquid and swell up, forming a pudding-like consistency. If you can, give it a stir once or twice during this time to break up any clumps.
3. **Prepare the Berries:** If using fresh berries, wash and slice them as needed. If you're using frozen berries, you can let them thaw in the fridge overnight or gently warm them in a saucepan over low heat to create a berry compote.
4. **Assemble the Pudding:** Once the chia pudding has set and is thick, give it a good stir. If it's too thick, you can adjust the consistency by adding a little more almond milk.
5. **Serve:** Spoon the chia pudding into serving glasses or bowls. Top with a generous layer of mixed berries. For an extra touch of elegance and flavor, garnish with additional berries and mint leaves.

Oatmeal with Almond Milk and Nuts

 2 servings    15 minutes

INGREDIENTS

- 1 cup rolled oats (use gluten-free oats if necessary)
- 2 cups almond milk (or any plant-based milk of your choice)
- A pinch of salt
- 1/2 teaspoon cinnamon (optional)
- 1 tablespoon maple syrup or sweetener of choice, adjust to taste
- 1/4 cup mixed nuts (such as almonds, walnuts, and pecans), roughly chopped
- Additional toppings: fresh fruits (like sliced banana, berries), chia seeds, flaxseeds, nut butter, or any other preferred toppings

DIRECTIONS

1. **Cook the Oatmeal:** In a medium saucepan, bring the almond milk to a boil. Add a pinch of salt and the rolled oats. Reduce the heat to a simmer and cook, stirring occasionally, for about 5-10 minutes or until the oats have absorbed the liquid and reached your desired consistency. If you like your oatmeal creamier, you might want to cook it for a shorter time; for a thicker consistency, cook it a bit longer.
2. **Add Flavors:** Once the oatmeal is nearly done, stir in the cinnamon and maple syrup. Adjust the sweetness according to your taste. If the oatmeal seems too thick, you can add a little more almond milk to loosen it.
3. **Toast the Nuts:** While the oatmeal is cooking, toast the chopped nuts in a dry skillet over medium heat for 2-3 minutes, or until they are fragrant and slightly golden. Be sure to keep an eye on them, as nuts can burn quickly. This step is optional but adds a lovely crunch and flavor.
4. **Serve:** Divide the cooked oatmeal into bowls. Top with the toasted nuts and any additional toppings of your choice.

Smoothie Bowl with Fresh Fruit

🍴 1 serving 🕐 10 minutes

INGREDIENTS

- 1 frozen banana, sliced
- 1/2 cup frozen berries (such as strawberries, blueberries, raspberries)
- 1/2 cup spinach or kale (optional, for a green boost)
- 1/2 avocado (for creaminess and healthy fats)
- 1/2 cup almond milk (or any plant-based milk of your choice)
- 1 tablespoon chia seeds or flaxseeds (for omega-3s and fiber)
- 1 tablespoon nut butter (almond, peanut, or cashew butter for added protein)
- 1 scoop protein powder (optional, for a protein boost)
- Toppings: Fresh fruits (banana slices, berry mix, kiwi slices), granola, coconut flakes, nuts, seeds, or a drizzle of honey or maple syrup

DIRECTIONS

1. **Blend the Smoothie:** In a blender, combine the frozen banana, frozen berries, leafy greens (if using), avocado, almond milk, chia or flaxseeds, nut butter, and protein powder (if using). Blend until smooth and creamy. Adjust the thickness by adding more almond milk if needed. The consistency should be thicker than a regular smoothie, as it will be eaten with a spoon.
2. **Prepare the Toppings:** While the smoothie is blending, prepare your chosen toppings. Slice any fresh fruits, gather the granola, nuts, seeds, and any other toppings you'd like to use.
3. **Assemble the Smoothie Bowl:** Pour the blended smoothie into a bowl. Arrange your toppings on the surface in a visually appealing way. You can create rows of different toppings or scatter them across the top.
4. **Serve Immediately:** Enjoy your smoothie bowl right away, while it's cold and fresh. Use a spoon to scoop up bites of the creamy smoothie along with the various toppings in each mouthful.

Vegan French Toast

 3-4 servings    20 minutes

INGREDIENTS

- 1 cup unsweetened almond milk (or any plant-based milk of your choice)
- 1/4 cup chickpea flour (for binding, similar to egg)
- 1 tablespoon nutritional yeast (for a slight umami flavor)
- 1 tablespoon maple syrup (plus more for serving)
- 1 teaspoon vanilla extract
- 1/2 teaspoon ground cinnamon
- 1/4 teaspoon ground nutmeg
- Pinch of salt
- 6-8 slices of thick bread (day-old bread works best)
- Vegan butter or oil for frying
- Toppings: Fresh fruit, vegan whipped cream, additional maple syrup, powdered sugar, or any other topping of your choice

DIRECTIONS

1. **Make the Batter:** In a shallow dish, whisk together the almond milk, chickpea flour, nutritional yeast, maple syrup, vanilla extract, cinnamon, nutmeg, and a pinch of salt until smooth. The mixture should resemble a traditional French toast batter in consistency; not too thick but able to coat the bread slices well.
2. **Prep the Bread:** Dip each slice of bread into the batter, allowing it to soak for a few seconds on each side. You don't want the bread to be soggy, just well-coated.
3. **Cook:** Heat a non-stick skillet or griddle over medium heat and add a little vegan butter or oil to coat the bottom. Once hot, place the batter-soaked bread slices on the skillet. Cook for about 3-4 minutes on each side, or until golden brown and slightly crispy.
4. **Serve:** Serve the vegan French toast hot, topped with your choice of fresh fruits, a dollop of vegan whipped cream, a drizzle of maple syrup, a sprinkle of powdered sugar, or any other toppings you enjoy.

Peanut Butter and Banana Smoothie

 2 smoothies    20 minutes

INGREDIENTS

- 2 ripe bananas, preferably frozen for a thicker smoothie
- 2 tablespoons peanut butter (choose a natural, unsweetened variety for a healthier option)
- 1 cup almond milk (or any plant-based milk of your choice)
- 1 tablespoon flaxseeds or chia seeds (optional, for added omega-3s and fiber)
- 1/2 teaspoon vanilla extract (optional, for enhanced flavor)
- A pinch of cinnamon (optional, for a bit of spice)
- Ice cubes (optional, if you're not using frozen bananas and want a colder smoothie)
- 1 scoop of vegan protein powder (optional, for a protein boost)

DIRECTIONS

1. **Prepare the Ingredients:** If you haven't frozen the bananas, peel and slice them. Freezing bananas in advance makes the smoothie creamier and serves as a natural ice substitute.
2. **Blend:** In a blender, combine the frozen bananas, peanut butter, almond milk, flaxseeds or chia seeds (if using), vanilla extract, cinnamon, and protein powder (if using). Add a few ice cubes if you like your smoothie extra cold and didn't use frozen bananas.
3. **Adjust Consistency:** Blend on high until smooth and creamy. If the smoothie is too thick, you can add a little more almond milk to reach your desired consistency. If it's too thin, add more frozen banana or ice.
4. **Serve:** Pour the smoothie into a glass and enjoy immediately. You can top it with a sprinkle of cinnamon, a few banana slices, or a drizzle of peanut butter for an extra treat.

Vegan Breakfast Burritos

 4 burritos   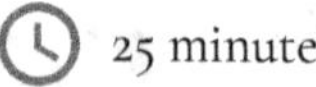 25 minutes

INGREDIENTS

- 4 large tortillas (ensure they're vegan)
- 1 (14 oz or 400g) package of firm tofu, drained and crumbled
- 1 tablespoon olive oil
- 1 teaspoon turmeric (for color and a health boost)
- 1/2 teaspoon garlic powder
- 1/2 teaspoon onion powder
- Salt and pepper to taste
- 1 cup black beans, rinsed and drained
- 1 avocado, sliced
- 1 cup fresh spinach or kale
- 1/2 cup diced tomatoes
- 1/4 cup chopped cilantro (optional)
- Vegan cheese shreds (optional)
- Salsa or hot sauce for serving
- Optional additions: sautéed mushrooms, bell peppers, onions, vegan sour cream, vegan sausage, or jalapeños

DIRECTIONS

1. **Prepare the Tofu Scramble:** Heat olive oil in a large skillet over medium heat. Add the crumbled tofu, turmeric, garlic powder, onion powder, salt, and pepper. Cook, stirring frequently, for about 5-7 minutes or until the tofu is heated through and slightly golden. The turmeric will give the tofu a bright, egg-like color.
2. **Warm the Tortillas:** Heat the tortillas in a dry skillet or microwave them for a few seconds until they are warm and flexible. This makes them easier to fold without tearing.
3. **Assemble the Burritos:** Lay out the warmed tortillas and evenly distribute the tofu scramble among them. Top each with black beans, avocado slices, spinach or kale, diced tomatoes, and cilantro. If using, sprinkle vegan cheese on top.
4. **Roll the Burritos:** Fold in the sides of each tortilla and roll them up tightly. If you're having trouble, you can look up techniques for folding burritos to ensure the fillings stay inside.
5. **Cook the Burritos (Optional):** For a crispy finish, heat a little more olive oil in the skillet and place the rolled burritos seam-side down. Cook until golden brown on all sides, turning gently, about 2 minutes per side.
6. **Serve:** Cut the burritos in half, if desired, and serve with salsa or hot sauce on the side for added flavor.

Almond Yogurt with Granola

 1 serving    5 minutes

INGREDIENTS

- 1 cup almond yogurt (plain or flavored, according to preference)
- 1/2 cup granola (choose a vegan brand or homemade)
- Fresh fruits for topping (berries, banana slices, kiwi, etc.)
- Optional toppings: chia seeds, flaxseeds, hemp seeds, nuts (almonds, walnuts, pecans), maple syrup, or agave nectar for extra sweetness

DIRECTIONS

1. **Choose Your Bowl:** Select a bowl for assembling your yogurt and granola dish.
2. **Add the Yogurt:** Spoon the almond yogurt into the bowl as the first layer. If you're using plain almond yogurt and prefer a little sweetness, you can stir in a bit of maple syrup or agave nectar to taste before adding it to the bowl.
3. **Layer the Granola:** Sprinkle the granola over the almond yogurt. The amount of granola can be adjusted based on your preference for crunch.
4. **Top with Fresh Fruits:** Add a generous layer of your chosen fresh fruits on top of the granola. The combination of fruits can vary according to season, availability, or personal preference. Berries, banana slices, and kiwi offer a nice mix of colors and flavors.
5. **Add Optional Toppings:** For added texture, nutrition, and flavor, sprinkle your choice of optional toppings over the fruits. Seeds and nuts not only add crunch but also a boost of omega-3 fatty acids, protein, and healthy fats.
6. **Serve Immediately:** Enjoy your almond yogurt with granola creation right away to ensure the granola remains crunchy and the fruits fresh.

Sweet Potato and Black Bean Hash

 4 servings    30 minutes

INGREDIENTS

- 2 medium sweet potatoes, peeled and diced into small cubes
- 1 can (15 oz) black beans, drained and rinsed
- 1 large onion, diced
- 1 bell pepper (any color), diced
- 2 cloves garlic, minced
- 2 tablespoons olive oil
- 1 teaspoon ground cumin
- 1/2 teaspoon smoked paprika (or regular paprika)
- Salt and pepper to taste
- Optional for serving: avocado slices, chopped fresh cilantro, lime wedges, hot sauce

DIRECTIONS

1. **Prep the Vegetables:** Peel and dice the sweet potatoes into small, even cubes to ensure they cook evenly. Dice the onion and bell pepper, and mince the garlic.
2. **Cook the Sweet Potatoes:** Heat the olive oil in a large skillet over medium heat. Add the diced sweet potatoes, season with a little salt and pepper, and cook for about 10 minutes, stirring occasionally, until they start to soften and get a bit golden on the edges.
3. **Add the Onion and Bell Pepper:** To the skillet, add the diced onion and bell pepper. Cook for an additional 5 minutes, or until the vegetables start to soften.
4. **Add Garlic and Spices:** Add the minced garlic, ground cumin, and smoked paprika to the skillet. Stir well to combine and cook for another minute until fragrant.
5. **Mix in Black Beans:** Add the drained and rinsed black beans to the skillet. Stir everything together and cook for another 5 minutes, or until everything is heated through and the sweet potatoes are fork-tender. Adjust the seasoning with more salt and pepper as needed.
6. **Serve:** Serve the hash hot, garnished with optional toppings like avocado slices, chopped fresh cilantro, a squeeze of lime juice, and a drizzle of hot sauce for an extra kick.

Vegan Sausages and Biscuits

🍴 6-8 sausages 🕐 55 minutes
8-10 biscuits 22 minutes

INGREDIENTS

Vegan Sausages:

- 1 cup vital wheat gluten
- 2 tablespoons nutritional yeast
- 1 teaspoon smoked paprika
- 1/2 teaspoon ground fennel seed
- 1/4 teaspoon black pepper
- 1/4 teaspoon red pepper flakes (optional, for heat)
- 1 teaspoon garlic powder
- 1 teaspoon onion powder
- 3/4 cup vegetable broth
- 2 tablespoons soy sauce
- 1 tablespoon olive oil
- 1 tablespoon tomato paste

Vegan Biscuits:

- 2 cups all-purpose flour
- 1 tablespoon baking powder
- 1/2 teaspoon baking soda
- 1/2 teaspoon salt
- 1/4 cup solid coconut oil or vegan butter
- 3/4 cup almond milk (or any plant-based milk)
- 1 tablespoon apple cider vinegar

DIRECTIONS

Vegan Sausages:

1. **Mix Dry Ingredients:** In a large bowl, whisk together vital wheat gluten, nutritional yeast, smoked paprika, ground fennel, black pepper, red pepper flakes, garlic powder, and onion powder.
2. **Combine Wet Ingredients:** In another bowl, mix vegetable broth, soy sauce, olive oil, and tomato paste.
3. **Form the Sausage Dough:** Pour the wet ingredients into the dry and stir until a dough forms. Knead the dough for a couple of minutes.
4. **Shape Sausages:** Divide the dough into equal portions and roll them into sausage shapes. Wrap each sausage tightly in aluminum foil.
5. **Steam:** Steam the wrapped sausages for 40 minutes. Once done, let them cool slightly before unwrapping. For extra flavor, you can brown the sausages in a skillet with a little oil.

Vegan Biscuits:

1. Preheat Oven: Preheat your oven to 450°F (230°C) and line a baking sheet with parchment paper.
2. Combine Dry Ingredients: In a large bowl, whisk together the flour, baking powder, baking soda, and salt.
3. Cut in Fat: Add the solid coconut oil or vegan butter to the flour mixture and use a pastry cutter or fork to cut it in until the mixture resembles coarse crumbs.
4. Make Vegan Buttermilk: Mix the almond milk with apple cider vinegar and let it sit for a few minutes to curdle.
5. Combine: Pour the vegan buttermilk into the flour mixture and stir until just combined. Do not overmix.
6. Shape Biscuits: Turn the dough out onto a lightly floured surface and pat it into a 1-inch thick layer. Use a biscuit cutter or glass to cut out biscuits. Re-form the dough scraps to make additional biscuits.
7. Bake: Place the biscuits on the prepared baking sheet and bake for 12-15 minutes, or until they are golden brown on top.

Matcha Green Tea Latte

 1 serving    10 minutes

INGREDIENTS

- 1 teaspoon matcha green tea powder
- 2 tablespoons hot water (not boiling, about 175°F or 80°C)
- 1 cup almond milk (or any plant-based milk of your choice)
- 1-2 teaspoons maple syrup or sweetener of choice (adjust to taste)
- Optional: A pinch of cinnamon or vanilla extract for extra flavor

DIRECTIONS

1. **Sift the Matcha:** Start by sifting the matcha powder into a bowl to remove any clumps. This ensures your latte will have a smooth texture.
2. **Whisk the Matcha:** Add the hot water to the matcha powder in the bowl. Using a bamboo whisk (chasen) or a small regular whisk, whisk vigorously in a zigzag motion until the matcha is fully dissolved and a light foam forms on the surface.
3. **Heat the Milk:** In a small saucepan, heat the almond milk over medium heat until hot but not boiling. Alternatively, you can heat the milk in the microwave. If you like froth in your latte, use a milk frother to froth the milk after heating.
4. **Sweeten:** Stir the maple syrup (or your chosen sweetener) into the heated milk. If you're using cinnamon or vanilla extract, add it to the milk as well.
5. **Combine:** Pour the matcha mixture into a mug, then gently pour in the heated, sweetened milk. Stir gently to combine.
6. **Serve:** If you frothed the milk, spoon any remaining foam on top. You can sprinkle a little matcha powder or cinnamon on top for decoration.

Apple Cinnamon Oat Bars

 9-12 bars  45 minutes

INGREDIENTS

- 2 cups rolled oats
- 1/2 cup whole wheat flour (or a gluten-free flour blend to make it gluten-free)
- 1/2 teaspoon baking powder
- 1/2 teaspoon baking soda
- 1/4 teaspoon salt
- 1 1/2 teaspoons ground cinnamon
- 1/4 teaspoon ground nutmeg
- 1/2 cup unsweetened applesauce
- 1/4 cup almond milk (or any plant-based milk)
- 1/3 cup maple syrup or agave nectar
- 1 teaspoon vanilla extract
- 1 large apple, peeled and finely diced
- 1/2 cup raisins or dried cranberries (optional)
- 1/4 cup chopped walnuts or pecans (optional)

DIRECTIONS

1. **Preheat Oven and Prep Pan:** Preheat your oven to 350°F (175°C). Line an 8x8 inch (20x20 cm) baking pan with parchment paper, leaving some overhang on the sides for easy removal.
2. **Mix Dry Ingredients:** In a large bowl, combine the rolled oats, whole wheat flour, baking powder, baking soda, salt, cinnamon, and nutmeg. Stir until well mixed.
3. **Combine Wet Ingredients:** In another bowl, whisk together the applesauce, almond milk, maple syrup (or agave), and vanilla extract until smooth.
4. **Combine Wet and Dry Mixtures:** Pour the wet ingredients into the bowl with the dry ingredients and stir until just combined. Be careful not to overmix.
5. **Add Apples and Optional Ingredients:** Fold in the diced apple, and if using, the raisins (or dried cranberries) and chopped nuts.
6. **Transfer to Pan and Bake:** Spread the mixture evenly in the prepared baking pan. Bake for 25-30 minutes, or until the top is golden and a toothpick inserted into the center comes out clean.
7. **Cool and Slice:** Allow the bars to cool in the pan on a wire rack for about 10 minutes, then use the parchment paper overhang to lift them out onto the rack to cool completely. Once cooled, slice into bars.

Pumpkin Spice Overnight Oats

🍴 2 servings ⏱ 8 hours

INGREDIENTS

- 1 cup rolled oats (gluten-free if necessary)
- 1 cup almond milk (or any plant-based milk of your choice)
- 1/2 cup pumpkin puree (not pumpkin pie filling)
- 2 tablespoons chia seeds
- 1-2 tablespoons maple syrup (adjust to taste)
- 1/2 teaspoon vanilla extract
- 1/2 teaspoon ground cinnamon
- 1/4 teaspoon ground nutmeg
- 1/8 teaspoon ground ginger
- 1/8 teaspoon ground cloves
- Pinch of salt
- Optional toppings: chopped nuts (such as pecans or walnuts), dried fruit, coconut flakes, a dollop of vegan yogurt, or extra drizzle of maple syrup

DIRECTIONS

1. **Mix the Ingredients**: In a mixing bowl or a mason jar, combine the rolled oats, almond milk, pumpkin puree, chia seeds, maple syrup, vanilla extract, cinnamon, nutmeg, ginger, cloves, and a pinch of salt. Stir well to ensure everything is evenly mixed.
2. **Refrigerate**: Cover the bowl or jar with a lid or plastic wrap. Refrigerate overnight, or for at least 6 hours, allowing the oats to soften and the flavors to meld together.
3. **Serve**: The next morning, give your pumpkin spice overnight oats a good stir. If the mixture is too thick, you can add a little more almond milk to reach your desired consistency.
4. **Add Toppings**: Top your overnight oats with your choice of nuts, dried fruits, coconut flakes, a dollop of vegan yogurt, or an extra drizzle of maple syrup for added sweetness and texture.
5. **Enjoy**: Enjoy your Pumpkin Spice Overnight Oats cold straight from the fridge or let it sit at room temperature for a few minutes if you prefer it slightly warmer.

Vegan Pear and Ginger Muffins

 12 muffins    40 minutes

INGREDIENTS

- 2 cups all-purpose flour (you can use whole wheat or a gluten-free blend for alternatives)
- 1/2 cup granulated sugar (adjust based on your sweetness preference)
- 1 tablespoon baking powder
- 1/2 teaspoon baking soda
- 1/2 teaspoon salt
- 1 teaspoon ground ginger
- 1/2 teaspoon cinnamon (optional, for added warmth)
- 1/3 cup unsweetened applesauce (as an egg replacer)
- 1 cup non-dairy milk (such as almond, soy, or oat milk)
- 1/4 cup vegetable oil or melted coconut oil
- 1 teaspoon vanilla extract
- 1 cup diced ripe pears (peeled or unpeeled based on preference)
- 1/4 cup crystallized ginger, finely chopped (for extra ginger flavor and texture)

DIRECTIONS

1. **Preheat the Oven**: Preheat your oven to 375°F (190°C). Line a muffin tin with paper liners or lightly grease it to prevent sticking.
2. **Combine Dry Ingredients**: In a large bowl, whisk together the flour, sugar, baking powder, baking soda, salt, ground ginger, and cinnamon (if using).
3. **Mix Wet Ingredients**: In another bowl, mix the applesauce, non-dairy milk, oil, and vanilla extract until well combined.
4. **Combine Wet and Dry Ingredients**: Pour the wet ingredients into the dry ingredients. Stir until just combined; it's important not to overmix to keep the muffins light and fluffy.
5. **Add Pears and Ginger**: Gently fold in the diced pears and crystallized ginger until evenly distributed throughout the batter.
6. **Fill the Muffin Tin**: Spoon the batter into the prepared muffin tin, filling each cup about 3/4 full.
7. **Bake**: Bake for 20-25 minutes, or until a toothpick inserted into the center of a muffin comes out clean.
8. **Cool**: Allow the muffins to cool in the tin for 5 minutes, then transfer them to a wire rack to cool completely.

Chickpea Flour Omelette with Vegetables

🍴 2 omelettes 🕐 18 minutes

INGREDIENTS

- 1 cup chickpea flour (also known as garbanzo bean flour)
- 1 1/4 cups water
- 1/4 teaspoon turmeric (for color and health benefits)
- 1/2 teaspoon baking powder (for fluffiness)
- 1/2 teaspoon salt
- 1/4 teaspoon black salt (kala namak, optional for an eggy flavor)
- 1/4 teaspoon black pepper
- 2 tablespoons nutritional yeast (for a cheesy flavor)
- 1/2 cup diced onions
- 1/2 cup diced bell peppers (any color)
- 1/2 cup chopped tomatoes
- 1/2 cup chopped spinach or kale
- 2 tablespoons chopped fresh herbs (such as parsley, cilantro, or chives)
- 1-2 tablespoons olive oil or any vegetable oil for cooking
- Optional: Vegan cheese, avocado slices, hot sauce for serving

DIRECTIONS

1. **Make the Batter**: In a mixing bowl, whisk together chickpea flour, water, turmeric, baking powder, salt, black salt (if using), black pepper, and nutritional yeast until smooth. Let the batter sit for about 5 minutes to thicken slightly.
2. **Prepare the Vegetables**: While the batter is resting, prepare your vegetables by dicing and chopping them to your liking.
3. **Mix Vegetables into Batter**: Add the onions, bell peppers, tomatoes, spinach (or kale), and fresh herbs to the batter. Stir until well combined.
4. **Cook the Omelette**: Heat a non-stick skillet or frying pan over medium heat and add a tablespoon of oil. Once hot, pour half of the batter into the pan, spreading it out to form a circle similar in size to a traditional omelette.
5. **Cook Until Golden**: Let the omelette cook for about 3-4 minutes, or until the edges start to lift and the bottom is golden brown. Carefully flip the omelette with a spatula and cook the other side for another 2-3 minutes.
6. **Serve**: Transfer the cooked omelette to a plate. If using, add vegan cheese and avocado slices on top, and fold the omelette in half. Serve hot with a side of hot sauce or any other condiments of your choice.

Cranberry and Orange Vegan Scones

🍴 8 scones 🕐 40 minutes

INGREDIENTS

- 2 cups all-purpose flour (for a gluten-free option, use a gluten-free all-purpose flour blend)
- 1/3 cup sugar (plus a little extra for sprinkling on top)
- 1 tablespoon baking powder
- 1/2 teaspoon salt
- 1/2 cup cold vegan butter (cut into small pieces)
- Zest of 1 orange
- 3/4 cup fresh cranberries (if using frozen, do not thaw)
- 3/4 cup full-fat coconut milk (or any plant-based milk), plus more for brushing on top
- 1 teaspoon vanilla extract

DIRECTIONS

1. **Preheat the Oven and Prepare Baking Sheet**: Preheat your oven to 400°F (200°C). Line a baking sheet with parchment paper.
2. **Mix Dry Ingredients**: In a large bowl, whisk together the flour, sugar, baking powder, and salt.
3. **Cut in Vegan Butter**: Add the cold vegan butter to the dry ingredients. Use a pastry cutter or your fingers to work the butter into the flour until the mixture resembles coarse crumbs. It's okay if some larger pieces of butter remain.
4. **Add Flavorings**: Stir in the orange zest and cranberries until they are evenly distributed throughout the flour mixture.
5. **Add Wet Ingredients**: Pour in the coconut milk and vanilla extract. Stir just until the dough comes together. Do not overmix.
6. **Form and Cut the Scones**: Turn the dough out onto a lightly floured surface. Gently shape it into a round disk about 1 inch thick. Using a sharp knife or a dough scraper, cut the disk into 8 equal wedges.
7. **Prepare for Baking**: Place the scones on the prepared baking sheet, leaving some space between each one. Brush the tops with a little coconut milk and sprinkle with a bit more sugar.
8. **Bake**: Bake in the preheated oven for 20-25 minutes, or until the scones are golden brown and a toothpick inserted into the center comes out clean.
9. **Cool**: Allow the scones to cool on the baking sheet for a few minutes, then transfer them to a wire rack to cool completely.

Vegan Cinnamon Apple Porridge

2 servings   25 minutes

INGREDIENTS

- 1 cup rolled oats (use gluten-free if necessary)
- 2 cups almond milk (or any plant-based milk of your choice)
- 1 large apple, peeled and diced
- 2 tablespoons maple syrup (adjust according to taste)
- 1/2 teaspoon ground cinnamon
- A pinch of salt
- Optional toppings: chopped nuts (such as walnuts or almonds), additional diced apple, a sprinkle of ground cinnamon, a drizzle of maple syrup, or a tablespoon of flaxseeds or chia seeds for extra nutrition

DIRECTIONS

1. **Cook the Apples:** In a medium-sized saucepan, combine the diced apples, maple syrup, cinnamon, and a splash of water. Cook over medium heat for about 5-7 minutes, or until the apples are soft and the mixture is somewhat syrupy.
2. **Add Oats and Milk:** To the same saucepan, add the rolled oats, almond milk, and a pinch of salt. Stir to combine.
3. **Simmer:** Bring the mixture to a simmer, then reduce the heat to low. Cook, stirring occasionally, for about 5-10 minutes, or until the porridge has thickened to your liking.
4. **Serve:** Once the porridge is cooked, remove it from the heat. Let it sit for a couple of minutes to cool down slightly and thicken a bit more.
5. **Add Toppings:** Serve the porridge in bowls, topped with your choice of additional diced apple, chopped nuts, a sprinkle of cinnamon, a drizzle of maple syrup, or flaxseeds/chia seeds.

Savory Vegan Breakfast Bowls with Quinoa

 2 servings    30 minutes

INGREDIENTS

- 1 cup quinoa (rinsed)
- 2 cups vegetable broth (or water)
- 1 tablespoon olive oil
- 1/2 cup diced red onion
- 1 cup sliced mushrooms
- 1 cup spinach or kale, roughly chopped
- 1 medium avocado, sliced
- 1/2 cup cherry tomatoes, halved
- 1/4 cup black beans, rinsed and drained
- 1/4 cup corn kernels (fresh, frozen, or canned)
- Salt and pepper, to taste
- Optional garnishes: chopped fresh cilantro, lime wedges, hot sauce, a drizzle of tahini, or nutritional yeast

DIRECTIONS

1. **Cook the Quinoa**: In a medium saucepan, bring the vegetable broth (or water) to a boil. Add the quinoa, reduce heat to low, cover, and simmer for about 15-20 minutes, or until all the liquid is absorbed and the quinoa is fluffy. Remove from heat and let it sit covered for 5 minutes. Fluff with a fork.
2. **Sauté the Vegetables**: While the quinoa is cooking, heat the olive oil in a skillet over medium heat. Add the diced onion and sauté for 2-3 minutes until translucent. Add the sliced mushrooms and cook for another 5 minutes until they are soft and browned. Add the spinach or kale and cook until just wilted. Season with salt and pepper to taste.
3. **Assemble the Bowls**: Divide the cooked quinoa among two bowls. Arrange the sautéed vegetables, avocado slices, cherry tomatoes, black beans, and corn kernels on top of the quinoa.
4. **Add Garnishes**: Finish each bowl with your choice of garnishes: chopped cilantro, a squeeze of lime juice, a drizzle of hot sauce or tahini, or a sprinkle of nutritional yeast for a cheesy flavor.

Vegan Cornmeal Pancakes with Maple Syrup

🍴 4 servings   🕐 30 minutes

INGREDIENTS

- 1 cup all-purpose flour (for a gluten-free option, you can use a gluten-free all-purpose flour blend)
- 1/2 cup cornmeal
- 2 tablespoons sugar (adjust according to taste)
- 1 tablespoon baking powder
- 1/2 teaspoon salt
- 1 and 1/4 cups almond milk (or any other plant-based milk)
- 1/4 cup water
- 2 tablespoons vegetable oil, plus more for cooking
- 1 teaspoon vanilla extract
- Maple syrup, for serving
- Optional: Fresh berries or sliced fruit for topping

DIRECTIONS

1. **Mix Dry Ingredients**: In a large bowl, whisk together the all-purpose flour, cornmeal, sugar, baking powder, and salt.
2. **Add Wet Ingredients**: In a separate bowl, combine the almond milk, water, vegetable oil, and vanilla extract. Mix well.
3. **Combine Wet and Dry Ingredients**: Pour the wet ingredients into the dry ingredients. Stir until just combined; it's okay if the batter is a little lumpy. Let the batter sit for 5 minutes to thicken slightly and allow the cornmeal to soften.
4. **Preheat the Pan**: Heat a non-stick skillet or griddle over medium heat. Brush with a little vegetable oil to prevent sticking.
5. **Cook the Pancakes**: Pour 1/4 cup of batter for each pancake onto the hot skillet. Cook until bubbles form on the surface of the pancake and the edges look set, about 2-3 minutes. Flip carefully and cook for another 2 minutes or until golden brown and cooked through.
6. **Serve**: Serve the pancakes hot, drizzled with maple syrup and topped with fresh berries or sliced fruit if desired.

Green Detox Smoothie with Spinach and Avocado

 2 smoothies  5 minutes

INGREDIENTS

- 1 cup fresh spinach leaves (tightly packed)
- 1/2 ripe avocado, peeled and pitted
- 1 small banana (preferably frozen for creaminess)
- 1/2 cup cucumber, chopped (peeled if not organic)
- 1 tablespoon chia seeds or flaxseeds (for added fiber and omega-3s)
- 1 tablespoon fresh lemon juice (about half a lemon)
- 1 cup coconut water or plain water (adjust for desired consistency)
- A few mint leaves (optional for extra freshness)
- 1/2 inch piece of ginger, peeled (optional for a zesty kick)
- Ice cubes (optional, if you prefer your smoothie colder)

DIRECTIONS

1. **Prepare Ingredients**: Make sure all your ingredients are washed, peeled, and ready to be blended. If you're using a frozen banana, ensure it's slightly thawed for easier blending.
2. **Blend Smoothie**: In a high-speed blender, combine the spinach, avocado, banana, cucumber, chia or flaxseeds, lemon juice, coconut water (or plain water), mint leaves, and ginger (if using). Blend on high until smooth and creamy. If the mixture is too thick, add a little more liquid until you reach your desired consistency.
3. **Adjust to Taste**: Taste the smoothie and adjust as necessary. If it's not sweet enough for you, you could add a small amount of maple syrup or honey (note: adding honey would make it non-vegan). If it's too thick, add more liquid.
4. **Serve Immediately**: Pour the smoothie into a glass, add ice cubes if desired, and enjoy immediately to benefit from the maximum amount of nutrients.

Turmeric and Ginger Infused Chai

INGREDIENTS

- 2 cups water
- 1 cup almond milk (or any plant-based milk of your choice)
- 1 inch fresh turmeric root, thinly sliced (or 1/2 teaspoon ground turmeric)
- 1 inch fresh ginger root, thinly sliced
- 2 cinnamon sticks (or 1/2 teaspoon ground cinnamon)
- 4-6 cardamom pods, lightly crushed
- 4 black peppercorns (optional, for added spice and to enhance turmeric absorption)
- 2-3 whole cloves
- 1-2 black tea bags (or 1-2 teaspoons loose black tea, depending on desired strength)
- Sweetener of choice (maple syrup, agave syrup, or stevia), to taste

DIRECTIONS

1. **Combine Spices and Water**: In a medium saucepan, combine the water, turmeric, ginger, cinnamon sticks, cardamom pods, black peppercorns (if using), and cloves. Bring the mixture to a boil.
2. **Simmer**: Reduce the heat and simmer gently for 10-15 minutes to allow the spices to infuse their flavors into the water.
3. **Add Tea and Milk**: Add the black tea bags (or loose tea) and almond milk to the saucepan. Return to a slight simmer, being careful not to let it boil vigorously to avoid curdling the milk. Simmer for an additional 5 minutes.
4. **Sweeten**: Remove the saucepan from the heat. Add your sweetener of choice to taste and stir until dissolved.
5. **Strain and Serve**: Strain the chai through a fine mesh strainer into cups or mugs to remove the spices and tea leaves.
6. **Enjoy**: Serve your Turmeric and Ginger Infused Chai hot. For an extra touch of warmth, you can sprinkle a little ground cinnamon or turmeric on top before serving.

Soups and Stews

Creamy Tomato Basil Soup

☆☆☆☆☆

 4-6 servings    40 minutes

INGREDIENTS

- 2 tablespoons olive oil
- 1 large onion, finely chopped
- 3 cloves garlic, minced
- 2 cans (14 oz each) diced tomatoes, with their juice
- 1/4 cup tomato paste
- 4 cups vegetable broth
- 1 cup canned coconut milk (full-fat for extra creaminess)
- 1/2 cup fresh basil leaves, chopped, plus more for garnish
- 1 teaspoon sugar (optional, to balance acidity)
- Salt and pepper, to taste
- Optional for serving: vegan cream or additional coconut milk, croutons, fresh basil leaves

DIRECTIONS

1. **Sauté the Aromatics:** In a large pot, heat the olive oil over medium heat. Add the chopped onion and sauté until soft and translucent, about 5 minutes. Add the minced garlic and cook for an additional minute, or until fragrant.
2. **Add Tomatoes:** Stir in the diced tomatoes (with their juice) and tomato paste. Cook for a few minutes to allow the flavors to meld together.
3. **Simmer:** Pour in the vegetable broth and bring the mixture to a simmer. Let it cook for about 20-25 minutes, stirring occasionally.
4. **Blend the Soup:** Carefully transfer the soup to a blender, working in batches if necessary, and blend until smooth. Alternatively, you can use an immersion blender directly in the pot. Return the soup to the pot if you used a stand blender.
5. **Add Coconut Milk and Basil:** Stir in the coconut milk and chopped basil. If you're using sugar, add it now. Heat the soup just until it's warm through; avoid boiling after adding the coconut milk to maintain the creamy texture.
6. **Season:** Taste and adjust the seasoning with salt and pepper. If the soup is too thick, you can thin it with a little extra vegetable broth or water.
7. **Serve:** Ladle the soup into bowls. Drizzle with a bit of vegan cream or additional coconut milk if desired, and garnish with croutons and fresh basil leaves.

Lentil and Vegetable Stew

🍴 4-6 servings   🕐 55 minutes

INGREDIENTS

- 1 cup dried green or brown lentils, rinsed and drained
- 2 tablespoons olive oil
- 1 large onion, chopped
- 2 carrots, peeled and diced
- 2 celery stalks, diced
- 3 cloves garlic, minced
- 1 teaspoon ground cumin
- 1/2 teaspoon ground coriander
- 1/2 teaspoon smoked paprika (optional, for a smoky flavor)
- 1 bay leaf
- 4 cups vegetable broth
- 1 can (14 oz) diced tomatoes, with their juice
- 2 medium potatoes, peeled and cubed
- 1 cup chopped kale or spinach
- Salt and pepper, to taste
- Fresh parsley, chopped (for garnish)
- Lemon wedges, for serving

DIRECTIONS

1. **Sauté the Aromatics:** In a large pot, heat the olive oil over medium heat. Add the onion, carrots, and celery, and cook until the vegetables are softened, about 5 minutes. Add the garlic, cumin, coriander, and smoked paprika, and cook for another minute until fragrant.

2. **Cook the Lentils:** Add the rinsed lentils to the pot along with the bay leaf, vegetable broth, and diced tomatoes (with their juice). Bring the mixture to a boil, then reduce the heat to low, cover, and simmer for about 20 minutes.

3. **Add Potatoes:** Stir in the cubed potatoes and continue to simmer, covered, for an additional 20 minutes, or until the potatoes and lentils are tender.

4. **Add Greens:** Once the lentils and potatoes are cooked, add the chopped kale or spinach to the pot. Stir until the greens have wilted and are heated through, about 2-3 minutes. Remove the bay leaf.

5. **Season and Serve:** Taste the stew and adjust the seasoning with salt and pepper as needed. Serve hot, garnished with fresh parsley and lemon wedges on the side.

Vegan Chili

 6-8 servings    60 minutes

INGREDIENTS

- 2 tablespoons olive oil
- 1 large onion, diced
- 2 cloves garlic, minced
- 1 bell pepper (any color), diced
- 2 carrots, peeled and diced
- 2 celery stalks, diced
- 1 zucchini, diced (optional)
- 1 jalapeño, seeded and finely chopped (optional, for heat)
- 1 tablespoon chili powder (adjust to taste)
- 1 teaspoon ground cumin
- 1 teaspoon smoked paprika
- 1/2 teaspoon dried oregano
- Salt and black pepper, to taste
- 1 can (28 oz) diced tomatoes, with their juice
- 1 can (15 oz) black beans, drained and rinsed
- 1 can (15 oz) kidney beans, drained and rinsed
- 1 can (15 oz) corn, drained (or equivalent frozen or fresh)
- 2 cups vegetable broth (adjust for desired thickness)
- 1 tablespoon tomato paste
- 1 teaspoon apple cider vinegar (optional, for a hint of tanginess)
- Fresh cilantro, chopped (for garnish)
- Avocado slices, lime wedges, vegan sour cream, and shredded vegan cheese (for serving)

DIRECTIONS

1. **Sauté the Vegetables:** In a large pot, heat the olive oil over medium heat. Add the onion, garlic, bell pepper, carrots, celery, zucchini (if using), and jalapeño (if using). Sauté until the vegetables are softened, about 5-7 minutes.
2. **Add the Spices:** Stir in the chili powder, cumin, smoked paprika, oregano, salt, and pepper. Cook for another minute until the spices are fragrant.
3. **Combine the Ingredients:** Add the diced tomatoes (with their juice), black beans, kidney beans, corn, vegetable broth, and tomato paste to the pot. Stir well to combine all the ingredients.
4. **Simmer:** Bring the mixture to a boil, then reduce the heat to low, cover, and let it simmer for at least 30 minutes, stirring occasionally. For a deeper flavor, you can let it simmer longer, up to an hour, if desired.
5. **Final Touches:** Before serving, stir in the apple cider vinegar (if using) and adjust the seasoning as needed. The vinegar adds a slight tanginess that can brighten up the flavors.
6. **Serve:** Ladle the chili into bowls and garnish with chopped fresh cilantro. Serve with avocado slices, lime wedges, vegan sour cream, and shredded vegan cheese on the side.

Butternut Squash Soup

 4-6 servings  60 minutes

INGREDIENTS

- 1 large butternut squash (about 2 to 3 pounds), peeled, seeded, and cut into cubes
- 2 tablespoons olive oil, divided
- Salt and pepper, to taste
- 1 large onion, diced
- 3 cloves garlic, minced
- 1 teaspoon ground ginger (or 1 tablespoon fresh ginger, minced)
- 1/2 teaspoon ground nutmeg
- 4 cups vegetable broth
- 1 can (14 oz) coconut milk (reserve a few tablespoons for garnish if desired)
- 2 tablespoons maple syrup or agave nectar (optional, to sweeten)
- Fresh herbs for garnish (such as thyme, parsley, or chives)

DIRECTIONS

1. **Roast the Squash:** Preheat your oven to 400°F (200°C). Toss the butternut squash cubes with 1 tablespoon olive oil, salt, and pepper. Spread them out on a baking sheet and roast for about 25-30 minutes, or until the squash is tender and caramelized.

2. **Sauté Aromatics:** While the squash is roasting, heat the remaining tablespoon of olive oil in a large pot over medium heat. Add the onion and sauté until it's translucent and slightly golden, about 5 minutes. Add the garlic, ginger, and nutmeg, and cook for another minute, until fragrant.

3. **Simmer:** Add the roasted butternut squash to the pot along with the vegetable broth. Bring the mixture to a boil, then reduce the heat and simmer for about 10-15 minutes to allow the flavors to meld.

4. **Blend the Soup:** Using an immersion blender, blend the soup directly in the pot until smooth. Alternatively, you can carefully transfer the soup to a blender, working in batches if necessary, and blend until smooth. Return the soup to the pot if you used a blender.

5. **Add Coconut Milk and Sweetener:** Stir in the coconut milk and maple syrup or agave nectar (if using). Heat the soup until it's warm throughout. Adjust the seasoning with additional salt and pepper to taste.

6. **Serve:** Ladle the soup into bowls. Drizzle with the reserved coconut milk and garnish with fresh herbs. Serve warm.

Mushroom and Barley Soup

🍴 6-8 servings 🕐 75 minutes

INGREDIENTS

- 1 cup pearl barley, rinsed
- 3 tablespoons olive oil
- 1 large onion, chopped
- 2 carrots, peeled and diced
- 2 celery stalks, diced
- 3 garlic cloves, minced
- 1 pound mushrooms (such as cremini, button, or a mix), cleaned and sliced
- 8 cups vegetable broth
- 2 bay leaves
- 1 teaspoon dried thyme (or 1 tablespoon fresh thyme leaves)
- Salt and pepper, to taste
- Fresh parsley, chopped (for garnish)

DIRECTIONS

1. **Prepare the Barley:** In a medium saucepan, bring water to a boil. Add the barley and simmer for about 30-40 minutes, or until tender. Drain any excess water and set aside.

2. **Sauté the Vegetables:** In a large pot, heat the olive oil over medium heat. Add the onion, carrots, and celery, and sauté until the vegetables start to soften, about 5 minutes. Add the garlic and cook for an additional minute, until fragrant.

3. **Cook the Mushrooms:** Add the sliced mushrooms to the pot and cook, stirring occasionally, until they release their moisture and begin to brown, about 10 minutes.

4. **Simmer the Soup:** Add the cooked barley, vegetable broth, bay leaves, and thyme to the pot. Bring to a boil, then reduce the heat and simmer for about 20 minutes to allow the flavors to meld. Season with salt and pepper to taste.

5. **Final Touches:** Remove the bay leaves. Taste and adjust the seasoning as needed. If the soup is too thick, you can add more broth or water to reach your desired consistency.

6. **Serve:** Ladle the soup into bowls and garnish with fresh parsley. Serve hot.

Sweet Potato and Coconut Milk Soup

 4-6 servings  45 minutes

INGREDIENTS

- 2 tablespoons coconut oil or olive oil
- 1 large onion, chopped
- 2 cloves garlic, minced
- 1 tablespoon grated ginger
- 2 large sweet potatoes, peeled and cubed
- 1 can (14 oz) coconut milk (full-fat for extra creaminess)
- 4 cups vegetable broth
- 1 teaspoon ground cumin
- 1/2 teaspoon ground coriander
- 1/4 teaspoon cayenne pepper (adjust to taste)
- Salt and pepper, to taste
- Juice of 1 lime
- Fresh cilantro, for garnish
- Toasted coconut flakes, for garnish (optional)

DIRECTIONS

1. **Sauté the Aromatics:** In a large pot, heat the coconut oil over medium heat. Add the onion and sauté until translucent, about 5 minutes. Add the garlic and grated ginger, and cook for another minute until fragrant.
2. **Cook the Sweet Potatoes:** Add the cubed sweet potatoes to the pot along with the ground cumin, ground coriander, and cayenne pepper. Stir to coat the sweet potatoes in the spices and cook for a couple of minutes.
3. **Simmer:** Pour in the coconut milk and vegetable broth. Bring the mixture to a boil, then reduce the heat to low, cover, and simmer for about 20-25 minutes, or until the sweet potatoes are tender.
4. **Blend the Soup:** Once the sweet potatoes are soft, use an immersion blender to blend the soup directly in the pot until smooth. Alternatively, you can carefully transfer the soup to a blender, working in batches if necessary, and blend until smooth. Return the soup to the pot if you used a stand blender.
5. **Season:** Add the lime juice to the blended soup and stir well. Season with salt and pepper to taste. If the soup is too thick, you can adjust the consistency by adding a little more vegetable broth or water.
6. **Serve:** Ladle the soup into bowls and garnish with fresh cilantro and toasted coconut flakes if desired.

Vegan Minestrone

 6-8 servings    45 minutes

INGREDIENTS

- 2 tablespoons olive oil
- 1 large onion, diced
- 2 carrots, peeled and diced
- 2 celery stalks, diced
- 3 cloves garlic, minced
- 1 zucchini, diced
- 1 cup green beans, trimmed and cut into 1/2-inch pieces
- 1 can (14 oz) diced tomatoes, with their juice
- 6 cups vegetable broth
- 1 can (14 oz) cannellini beans (or any white beans), drained and rinsed
- 1 teaspoon dried oregano
- 1 teaspoon dried basil
- Salt and pepper, to taste
- 1 cup small pasta shapes (e.g., ditalini, elbows, or small shells), use gluten-free pasta if necessary
- 2 cups baby spinach or kale, roughly chopped
- Fresh parsley, chopped, for garnish
- Vegan Parmesan cheese, for serving (optional)

DIRECTIONS

1. **Sauté the Base Vegetables:** In a large pot, heat the olive oil over medium heat. Add the onion, carrots, and celery, and sauté until the vegetables begin to soften, about 5 minutes. Add the garlic and cook for another minute until fragrant.
2. **Add Zucchini and Green Beans:** Stir in the zucchini and green beans, and continue cooking for a few more minutes.
3. **Add Tomatoes and Broth:** Pour in the diced tomatoes (with their juice) and vegetable broth. Bring the mixture to a simmer.
4. **Season:** Add the cannellini beans, dried oregano, and dried basil. Season with salt and pepper to taste. Simmer for about 15 minutes to let the flavors meld together.
5. **Cook the Pasta:** Add the pasta to the pot and cook according to the package instructions until al dente, usually about 8-10 minutes, depending on the type of pasta.
6. **Add Greens:** Stir in the spinach or kale, and cook just until the greens have wilted, about 2 minutes.
7. **Serve:** Ladle the minestrone into bowls, garnish with fresh parsley, and if desired, sprinkle with vegan Parmesan cheese.

Spicy Black Bean Soup

 6-8 servings  45 minutes

INGREDIENTS

- 2 tablespoons olive oil
- 1 large onion, chopped
- 2 carrots, peeled and diced
- 2 celery stalks, diced
- 4 garlic cloves, minced
- 2 teaspoons ground cumin
- 1 teaspoon chili powder (adjust to taste for spice level)
- 1/2 teaspoon smoked paprika
- 1/4 teaspoon cayenne pepper (optional, for extra heat)
- 4 cans (15 oz each) black beans, drained and rinsed
- 4 cups vegetable broth
- 1 can (14.5 oz) diced tomatoes, with their juice
- 2 tablespoons tomato paste
- Salt and black pepper, to taste
- Juice of 1 lime
- Fresh cilantro, chopped, for garnish
- Diced avocado, sliced jalapeños, vegan sour cream, and tortilla chips, for serving

DIRECTIONS

1. **Sauté the Vegetables:** In a large pot, heat the olive oil over medium heat. Add the onion, carrots, and celery. Cook, stirring occasionally, until the vegetables are softened, about 5-7 minutes. Add the minced garlic, cumin, chili powder, smoked paprika, and cayenne pepper. Cook for another minute, until fragrant.
2. **Add Beans and Liquids:** Stir in the black beans, vegetable broth, diced tomatoes (with their juice), and tomato paste. Bring to a simmer, then reduce the heat to low, cover, and let it cook for about 30 minutes to allow the flavors to meld.
3. **Blend (Optional):** For a creamier texture, use an immersion blender to partially blend the soup directly in the pot, or carefully transfer about half of the soup to a blender, blend until smooth, and then mix it back into the pot. Leave some beans whole for texture.
4. **Season:** Stir in the lime juice and season with salt and black pepper to taste. Let the soup cook for another 5 minutes, adjusting the seasoning as needed.
5. **Serve:** Ladle the soup into bowls and garnish with chopped cilantro. Serve with diced avocado, sliced jalapeños, vegan sour cream, and tortilla chips on the side.

Moroccan Chickpea Soup

 4-6 servings    50 minutes

INGREDIENTS

- 2 tablespoons olive oil
- 1 large onion, chopped
- 2 garlic cloves, minced
- 2 carrots, peeled and diced
- 2 celery stalks, diced
- 1 teaspoon ground cumin
- 1/2 teaspoon ground turmeric
- 1/2 teaspoon ground cinnamon
- 1/4 teaspoon cayenne pepper (adjust to taste)
- Salt and black pepper, to taste
- 1 can (14 oz) diced tomatoes, with their juice
- 4 cups vegetable broth
- 1 can (15 oz) chickpeas, drained and rinsed
- 1 cup green lentils, rinsed
- 1 large sweet potato, peeled and cubed
- 1/2 cup chopped dried apricots (optional, for sweetness and texture)
- 1 zucchini, diced
- Juice of 1 lemon
- Fresh cilantro or parsley, chopped, for garnish

DIRECTIONS

1. **Sauté the Aromatics:** In a large pot, heat the olive oil over medium heat. Add the onion, garlic, carrots, and celery. Cook, stirring occasionally, until the vegetables are softened, about 5 minutes.
2. **Spice It Up:** Add the cumin, turmeric, cinnamon, cayenne pepper, salt, and black pepper to the pot. Stir well to coat the vegetables in the spices, and cook for another minute until fragrant.
3. **Add Tomatoes, Broth, and Legumes:** Pour in the diced tomatoes (with their juice), vegetable broth, chickpeas, lentils, and sweet potato cubes. Bring to a boil, then reduce the heat, cover, and simmer for about 25 minutes, or until the lentils and sweet potatoes are tender.
4. **Add Zucchini and Apricots:** Stir in the diced zucchini and chopped dried apricots (if using). Continue to simmer for another 10 minutes, or until the zucchini is tender.
5. **Finish with Lemon Juice:** Once all the vegetables are cooked and the soup has thickened, remove from heat and stir in the lemon juice. Adjust the seasoning with more salt, pepper, or spices to taste.
6. **Serve:** Ladle the soup into bowls and garnish with fresh cilantro or parsley. Serve hot.

Thai Green Curry with Tofu

🍴 4 servings 🕐 30 minutes

INGREDIENTS

- 14 oz (400g) firm tofu, pressed and cubed
- 2 tablespoons coconut oil (or vegetable oil)
- 2-3 tablespoons green curry paste (adjust based on spice preference)
- 1 can (14 oz or 400 ml) coconut milk
- 1 cup vegetable broth
- 1 tablespoon soy sauce (or tamari for gluten-free option)
- 1 tablespoon maple syrup (or sugar)
- 1 red bell pepper, sliced
- 1 zucchini, sliced
- 1 cup snap peas or green beans
- 1/2 cup bamboo shoots (optional)
- 1/4 cup fresh basil leaves, chopped
- 2 tablespoons lime juice
- Salt to taste
- Steamed jasmine rice or rice noodles, for serving

DIRECTIONS

1. **Prepare the Tofu:** After pressing the tofu to remove excess water, cut it into cubes. Heat 1 tablespoon of coconut oil in a pan over medium heat and fry the tofu cubes until golden brown on all sides. Remove from the pan and set aside.
2. **Cook the Curry:** In the same pan, add another tablespoon of coconut oil and the green curry paste. Fry for a minute until fragrant. Slowly pour in the coconut milk and vegetable broth, stirring well to combine the curry paste with the liquids.
3. **Add Vegetables and Tofu:** Add the soy sauce and maple syrup to the pan, stirring well. Then add the sliced bell pepper, zucchini, snap peas (or green beans), and bamboo shoots (if using). Bring the mixture to a gentle simmer and let cook for about 5-7 minutes, or until the vegetables are just tender.
4. **Final Touches:** Add the fried tofu cubes back into the pan. Stir in the chopped basil and lime juice. Taste and adjust seasoning with salt or more soy sauce if needed.
5. **Serve:** Serve the curry hot over steamed jasmine rice or alongside rice noodles. Garnish with additional basil leaves if desired.

Roasted Red Pepper and Tomato Soup

☆☆☆☆☆

4 servings · 70 minutes

INGREDIENTS

- 4 large red bell peppers
- 1 tablespoon olive oil, plus more for drizzling on the peppers
- 1 large onion, chopped
- 3 cloves garlic, minced
- 1 (28-ounce) can of whole tomatoes (with their juice)
- 2 cups vegetable broth
- 1 teaspoon smoked paprika
- 1 teaspoon dried oregano
- Salt and pepper, to taste
- A pinch of red pepper flakes (optional, for heat)
- Fresh basil leaves, for garnish
- Coconut cream or vegan sour cream, for serving (optional)

DIRECTIONS

1. **Roast the Peppers**: Preheat your oven to 450°F (230°C). Place the whole red bell peppers on a baking sheet and drizzle with a little olive oil. Roast in the oven for 25-30 minutes, turning occasionally, until the skins are charred and blistered. Remove from the oven and place the peppers in a bowl, covering with plastic wrap to steam for about 10 minutes. Once cool enough to handle, peel off the skins, remove the seeds, and chop the peppers.

2. **Sauté the Aromatics**: In a large pot, heat 1 tablespoon of olive oil over medium heat. Add the chopped onion and sauté until translucent, about 5 minutes. Add the minced garlic and cook for another minute until fragrant.

3. **Add Tomatoes and Peppers**: Stir in the whole tomatoes (breaking them up with your spoon), roasted red peppers, vegetable broth, smoked paprika, oregano, salt, pepper, and red pepper flakes (if using). Bring to a simmer.

4. **Simmer the Soup**: Let the soup simmer for 20-25 minutes, allowing the flavors to meld together.

5. **Blend the Soup**: Use an immersion blender to puree the soup directly in the pot until smooth. Alternatively, you can transfer the soup to a blender and blend in batches, then return it to the pot.

6. **Adjust Seasonings**: Taste and adjust the seasoning as needed, adding more salt, pepper, or spices according to your preference.

7. **Serve**: Ladle the soup into bowls and garnish with fresh basil leaves. If desired, add a swirl of coconut cream or a dollop of vegan sour cream for extra creaminess.

Vegan French Onion Soup

☆☆☆☆☆

4-6 servings · 80 minutes

INGREDIENTS

- 4 large yellow onions, thinly sliced
- 3 tablespoons olive oil or vegan butter
- 2 cloves garlic, minced
- 1 teaspoon sugar (optional, to help with caramelization)
- 1/2 cup dry white wine (ensure it's vegan)
- 6 cups vegetable broth
- 2 tablespoons soy sauce or tamari (for depth of flavor)
- 1 bay leaf
- 1 teaspoon dried thyme (or a few sprigs of fresh thyme)
- Salt and pepper, to taste
- 4-6 slices of crusty bread (ensure it's vegan)
- 1-2 cups shredded vegan cheese (Gruyère style if available)

DIRECTIONS

1. **Caramelize the Onions**: In a large pot, heat the olive oil or vegan butter over medium heat. Add the onions and cook, stirring occasionally, for about 25-30 minutes until they are deeply caramelized. If they start to stick, you can add a splash of water. Halfway through, sprinkle the sugar to help with the caramelization process.
2. **Deglaze with Wine**: Add the minced garlic to the onions and cook for another 1-2 minutes until fragrant. Pour in the white wine to deglaze the pot, scraping up any browned bits from the bottom. Allow the wine to reduce by half.
3. **Add Broth and Seasonings**: Stir in the vegetable broth, soy sauce or tamari, bay leaf, and thyme. Bring the mixture to a simmer and let it cook for another 20-30 minutes. Season with salt and pepper to taste.
4. **Prep the Bread**: While the soup simmers, toast the slices of bread. You can do this in the oven under the broiler or in a toaster until lightly golden and crispy.
5. **Assemble and Broil**: Preheat your oven's broiler. Ladle the soup into oven-safe bowls, place a slice of toasted bread on top of each, and generously cover with shredded vegan cheese. Place the bowls on a baking sheet for stability and broil for a few minutes until the cheese is melted and bubbly. Keep an eye on it to prevent burning.
6. **Serve**: Carefully remove the bowls from the oven (they will be hot), garnish with a little fresh thyme if desired, and serve immediately.

White Bean and Kale Stew

 4-6 servings    50 minutes

INGREDIENTS

- 2 tablespoons olive oil
- 1 large onion, chopped
- 3 garlic cloves, minced
- 2 carrots, diced
- 2 celery stalks, diced
- 1 teaspoon dried thyme
- 1/2 teaspoon dried rosemary
- 1/4 teaspoon red pepper flakes (optional, for heat)
- 4 cups vegetable broth
- 2 cans (15 oz each) white beans (such as cannellini or great northern), rinsed and drained
- 1 bunch kale, stems removed and leaves roughly chopped
- Salt and pepper, to taste
- Juice of 1 lemon
- Fresh parsley, chopped, for garnish

DIRECTIONS

1. **Sauté Aromatics**: In a large pot, heat the olive oil over medium heat. Add the onion and sauté until it becomes translucent, about 5 minutes. Add the garlic, carrots, and celery, cooking for another 5 minutes until the vegetables start to soften.
2. **Add Herbs and Spices**: Stir in the thyme, rosemary, and red pepper flakes (if using), cooking for a minute until fragrant.
3. **Add Broth and Beans**: Pour in the vegetable broth and add the rinsed white beans. Bring the mixture to a simmer, then reduce the heat to low. Simmer for about 15-20 minutes to allow the flavors to meld together.
4. **Add Kale**: Stir in the chopped kale, and continue to simmer until the kale is wilted and tender, about 5-10 minutes. The heat from the stew will soften the kale without overcooking it, preserving its nutrients.
5. **Season**: Add the lemon juice, and season the stew with salt and pepper to taste. The lemon juice will brighten the flavors and add a slight tanginess to the stew.
6. **Serve**: Ladle the stew into bowls and garnish with chopped fresh parsley. Serve hot.

Vegan Gumbo with Okra and Vegetables

 4-6 servings    60 minutes

INGREDIENTS

- 2 tablespoons olive oil
- 1 large onion, diced
- 3 celery stalks, diced
- 1 green bell pepper, diced
- 4 cloves garlic, minced
- 1 cup sliced okra (fresh or frozen)
- 1 can (14.5 oz) diced tomatoes
- 4 cups vegetable broth
- 2 bay leaves
- 1 teaspoon smoked paprika
- 1 teaspoon dried thyme
- 1/2 teaspoon cayenne pepper (adjust to taste)
- 1/2 teaspoon ground black pepper
- 1 teaspoon file powder (optional, for authentic gumbo flavor)
- 1 cup sliced fresh mushrooms (optional)
- 1 can (15 oz) red kidney beans, rinsed and drained
- Salt to taste
- Cooked rice, for serving
- Sliced green onions and chopped parsley, for garnish

DIRECTIONS

1. **Sauté Vegetables**: In a large pot or Dutch oven, heat the olive oil over medium heat. Add the onion, celery, and bell pepper. Sauté until the vegetables are softened, about 5-7 minutes. Add the garlic and cook for an additional minute until fragrant.
2. **Add Okra and Tomatoes**: Stir in the okra and diced tomatoes (with their juice). Cook for a few minutes until the okra starts to soften.
3. **Add Liquids and Spices**: Pour in the vegetable broth. Add the bay leaves, smoked paprika, thyme, cayenne pepper, black pepper, and file powder (if using). Bring to a simmer.
4. **Simmer**: Reduce heat to low and let the gumbo simmer for about 30 minutes. If you're adding mushrooms, include them at this point. The gumbo should start to thicken slightly.
5. **Add Beans**: Stir in the kidney beans and continue to simmer for another 10 minutes. Taste and adjust seasoning with salt and additional spices as needed.
6. **Serve**: Remove the bay leaves. Serve the gumbo hot over cooked rice, garnished with sliced green onions and chopped parsley.

Curried Cauliflower and Chickpea Soup

 4 servings

 45 minutes

INGREDIENTS

- 2 tablespoons olive oil
- 1 large onion, chopped
- 3 cloves garlic, minced
- 1 tablespoon grated ginger
- 1 tablespoon curry powder (adjust according to taste and preferred spice level)
- 1 teaspoon ground turmeric
- 1/2 teaspoon ground cumin
- 1 medium head of cauliflower, cut into florets
- 1 can (15 oz) chickpeas, rinsed and drained
- 4 cups vegetable broth
- 1 can (14 oz) coconut milk (light or full-fat, based on preference)
- Salt and pepper, to taste
- Juice of 1 lime
- Fresh cilantro, chopped, for garnish
- Additional toppings (optional): A dollop of vegan yogurt, toasted nuts or seeds, chili flakes

DIRECTIONS

1. **Sauté Aromatics**: In a large pot, heat the olive oil over medium heat. Add the onion and sauté until it becomes translucent and soft, about 5 minutes. Add the garlic and ginger, cooking for another minute until fragrant.
2. **Add Spices**: Stir in the curry powder, turmeric, and cumin. Cook for a minute until the spices are well combined and aromatic, being careful not to let them burn.
3. **Combine Vegetables and Chickpeas**: Add the cauliflower florets and chickpeas to the pot, stirring to coat them in the spice mixture.
4. **Add Broth and Simmer**: Pour in the vegetable broth and bring the mixture to a boil. Reduce the heat to a simmer, cover, and cook for about 20 minutes, or until the cauliflower is tender.
5. **Add Coconut Milk**: Stir in the coconut milk and continue to cook for another 5 minutes, letting the soup gently simmer.
6. **Blend (Optional)**: For a smoother soup, use an immersion blender to partially or completely blend the soup to your desired consistency. You can also leave it chunky if you prefer.
7. **Season and Serve**: Remove from heat and stir in the lime juice. Season with salt and pepper to taste. Serve the soup hot, garnished with chopped cilantro and any additional toppings you like.

Vegan Pho with Tofu and Mushrooms

 4 servings    45 minutes

INGREDIENTS

For the Broth:

- 8 cups vegetable broth
- 1 large onion, peeled and halved
- 4 cloves of garlic, peeled and smashed
- 1 3-inch piece of ginger, sliced
- 2 cinnamon sticks
- 3 star anise
- 4 cloves
- 1 cardamom pod (optional)
- 1 tablespoon soy sauce or tamari
- 1 tablespoon maple syrup or sugar

For the Soup:

- 8 oz rice noodles
- 1 block (14 oz) firm tofu, pressed and cut into cubes
- 8 oz mushrooms (such as shiitake or cremini), sliced
- 1 tablespoon oil (for sautéing mushrooms)
- Salt, to taste

Toppings:

- Bean sprouts
- Thinly sliced green onions
- Fresh cilantro
- Fresh mint
- Fresh basil (Thai basil if available)
- Lime wedges

DIRECTIONS

1. **Prepare the Broth**: In a large pot, combine the vegetable broth, onion, garlic, ginger, cinnamon sticks, star anise, cloves, cardamom pod (if using), soy sauce, and maple syrup. Bring to a boil, then reduce heat and simmer, covered, for 25-30 minutes to allow the flavors to infuse.

2. **Cook Noodles**: Cook the rice noodles according to package instructions, then rinse under cold water and drain. Set aside.

3. **Prepare Tofu and Mushrooms**: While the broth is simmering, heat oil in a pan over medium heat. Sauté the mushrooms until they release their moisture and become golden brown. Season with a little salt. In the same or a different pan, lightly fry the tofu cubes until all sides are golden and crispy. Set aside.

4. **Strain the Broth**: After the broth has simmered, strain it through a fine-mesh sieve into another pot. Discard the solids. Taste the broth and adjust the seasoning with more soy sauce or salt if needed.

5. **Assemble the Pho**: Divide the cooked noodles among serving bowls. Top with sautéed mushrooms, tofu cubes, and pour the hot broth over them.

6. **Add Toppings**: Serve the pho with a platter of bean sprouts, green onions, cilantro, mint, basil, lime wedges, and sliced chili peppers on the side, allowing everyone to add their preferred toppings. Offer hoisin sauce and sriracha for additional flavoring.

Sweet Corn and Zucchini Chowder

 4 servings    45 minutes

INGREDIENTS

- 2 tablespoons olive oil
- 1 large onion, diced
- 2 cloves garlic, minced
- 2 medium zucchinis, diced
- 4 cups fresh corn kernels (from about 4-5 ears of corn)
- 1 large potato, peeled and diced
- 4 cups vegetable broth
- 1 cup unsweetened almond milk (or any plant-based milk)
- 1 teaspoon fresh thyme leaves (or ½ teaspoon dried thyme)
- Salt and pepper, to taste
- 1/4 teaspoon smoked paprika (optional, for a smoky flavor)
- Fresh chives or parsley, chopped, for garnish

DIRECTIONS

1. **Sauté the Onion and Garlic**: In a large pot, heat the olive oil over medium heat. Add the onion and garlic, and sauté until the onion is translucent and soft, about 5 minutes.
2. **Add Zucchini and Corn**: Add the diced zucchini and corn kernels to the pot. Cook for another 5-7 minutes, until the vegetables start to soften slightly.
3. **Add Potato and Broth**: Stir in the diced potato and vegetable broth. Bring the mixture to a boil, then reduce the heat to low and simmer, covered, until the potato is tender, about 15-20 minutes.
4. **Blend for Creaminess**: Once the potatoes are soft, use an immersion blender to partially blend the soup directly in the pot. Aim to puree about half of the soup to thicken it while leaving the rest chunky for texture. If you don't have an immersion blender, transfer about half of the soup to a blender, carefully blend until smooth, and then stir it back into the pot.
5. **Add Plant-Based Milk and Seasonings**: Stir in the almond milk, thyme, salt, pepper, and smoked paprika (if using). Let the soup simmer for another 5 minutes to meld the flavors. Adjust seasoning as needed.
6. **Serve**: Ladle the chowder into bowls and garnish with chopped chives or parsley.

Vegan Pozole with Hominy and Peppers

4-6 servings   55 minutes

INGREDIENTS

- 2 tablespoons olive oil
- 1 large onion, diced
- 3 cloves garlic, minced
- 2 poblano peppers, seeded and diced
- 1 red bell pepper, seeded and diced
- 1 jalapeño pepper, seeded and minced (optional, for extra heat)
- 2 teaspoons ground cumin
- 1 teaspoon dried oregano
- 1/2 teaspoon smoked paprika
- 4 cups vegetable broth
- 2 cans (15 oz each) hominy, drained and rinsed
- 1 can (14.5 oz) diced tomatoes, with juice
- 1 cup frozen corn, thawed
- Salt and pepper, to taste
- Juice of 1 lime
- Fresh cilantro, chopped, for garnish
- Diced avocado, sliced radishes, and lime wedges, for serving

DIRECTIONS

1. **Sauté Aromatics**: In a large pot, heat the olive oil over medium heat. Add the onion and garlic, and sauté until the onion is translucent and softened, about 5 minutes.
2. **Add Peppers and Spices**: Stir in the poblano peppers, red bell pepper, jalapeño pepper (if using), ground cumin, dried oregano, and smoked paprika. Cook, stirring occasionally, for another 5-7 minutes until the peppers are softened.
3. **Add Broth and Hominy**: Pour in the vegetable broth, then add the drained hominy and diced tomatoes with their juice. Stir to combine everything well.
4. **Simmer the Pozole**: Bring the mixture to a boil, then reduce the heat to low and let it simmer, partially covered, for about 25-30 minutes to allow the flavors to meld together.
5. **Add Corn**: Add the thawed corn to the pot, and continue to simmer for an additional 5 minutes.
6. **Season**: Remove the pozole from the heat and stir in the lime juice. Season with salt and pepper to taste.
7. **Serve**: Ladle the pozole into bowls and garnish with chopped fresh cilantro. Serve with diced avocado, sliced radishes, and lime wedges on the side.

Moroccan Lentil and Sweet Potato Stew

 4-6 servings  55 minutes

INGREDIENTS

- 2 tablespoons olive oil
- 1 large onion, diced
- 3 cloves garlic, minced
- 1 tablespoon grated ginger
- 2 teaspoons ground cumin
- 1 teaspoon ground coriander
- 1/2 teaspoon ground cinnamon
- 1/4 teaspoon ground turmeric
- 1/4 teaspoon cayenne pepper (adjust according to taste)
- 1 large sweet potato, peeled and cubed (about 2 cups)
- 1 cup dried lentils (green, brown, or red), rinsed
- 4 cups vegetable broth
- 1 can (14.5 oz) diced tomatoes, with their juice
- 1 teaspoon salt (adjust to taste)
- 1/2 teaspoon black pepper
- 1 can (15 oz) chickpeas, drained and rinsed
- 2 cups baby spinach or chopped kale
- Juice of 1 lemon
- Fresh cilantro, chopped, for garnish

DIRECTIONS

1. **Sauté Aromatics**: In a large pot or Dutch oven, heat the olive oil over medium heat. Add the onion, and sauté until translucent, about 5 minutes. Add the garlic and ginger, cooking for another minute until fragrant.
2. **Add Spices**: Stir in the cumin, coriander, cinnamon, turmeric, and cayenne pepper. Cook for about 1 minute until the spices are well combined and aromatic.
3. **Add Sweet Potato and Lentils**: Add the cubed sweet potato and rinsed lentils to the pot. Stir to coat them in the spice mixture.
4. **Pour in Broth and Tomatoes**: Add the vegetable broth and diced tomatoes with their juice. Bring the mixture to a boil, then reduce the heat to low, cover, and simmer for about 25-30 minutes, or until the lentils and sweet potatoes are tender.
5. **Add Chickpeas and Greens**: Stir in the chickpeas and spinach (or kale). Cook for another 5 minutes, or until the greens have wilted and the chickpeas are heated through.
6. **Season**: Remove the pot from the heat. Stir in the lemon juice, and adjust the seasoning with salt and pepper to taste.
7. **Serve**: Ladle the stew into bowls, and garnish with fresh chopped cilantro. Serve hot.

Salads

Quinoa Tabbouleh

 4-6 servings  45 minutes

INGREDIENTS

- 1 cup quinoa
- 2 cups water
- 1/4 cup olive oil
- 1/4 cup lemon juice (about 2 lemons)
- 2 cups fresh parsley, finely chopped
- 1 cup fresh mint, finely chopped
- 3 medium tomatoes, diced
- 1 cucumber, diced
- 3 green onions, thinly sliced
- Salt and pepper, to taste

DIRECTIONS

1. **Cook Quinoa:** Rinse the quinoa under cold water in a fine-mesh strainer. In a medium saucepan, bring 2 cups of water to a boil. Add the quinoa, reduce the heat to low, cover, and simmer for about 15 minutes, or until the quinoa is cooked and the water is absorbed. Fluff with a fork and let it cool to room temperature. You can also spread the cooked quinoa on a baking sheet to cool faster.

2. **Prepare the Dressing:** In a small bowl, whisk together the olive oil and lemon juice. Season with salt and pepper to taste. Adjust the seasoning according to your preference.

3. **Combine the Salad:** In a large bowl, combine the cooled quinoa, chopped parsley, mint, diced tomatoes, diced cucumber, and sliced green onions.

4. **Dress the Salad:** Pour the dressing over the salad and toss to combine thoroughly. Adjust the salt and pepper as needed.

5. **Chill:** For the best flavor, let the tabbouleh chill in the refrigerator for at least 30 minutes before serving. This allows the flavors to meld together.

6. **Serve:** Serve the quinoa tabbouleh cold or at room temperature. It can be enjoyed on its own, as a side dish, or as part of a mezze platter.

Avocado and Black Bean Salad

 4-6 servings  20 minutes

INGREDIENTS

- 2 ripe avocados, diced
- 1 can (15 oz) black beans, rinsed and drained
- 1 red bell pepper, diced
- 1/2 red onion, finely chopped
- 1 cup corn (fresh, frozen and thawed, or canned and drained)
- 1/4 cup fresh cilantro, chopped
- For the Lime Dressing:
- 1/4 cup olive oil
- 2 tablespoons lime juice (about 1 lime)
- 1 garlic clove, minced
- 1/2 teaspoon ground cumin
- Salt and pepper, to taste

DIRECTIONS

1. **Prepare the Salad Ingredients:** In a large bowl, combine the diced avocados, rinsed black beans, diced red bell pepper, chopped red onion, corn, and chopped cilantro. Gently toss to mix the ingredients.
2. **Make the Lime Dressing:** In a small bowl, whisk together the olive oil, lime juice, minced garlic, ground cumin, salt, and pepper until well combined.
3. **Dress the Salad:** Pour the lime dressing over the salad ingredients. Gently toss everything together to ensure the salad is evenly coated with the dressing. Be careful not to mash the avocados.
4. **Chill:** For the best flavor, let the salad chill in the refrigerator for about 30 minutes before serving. This step is optional but allows the flavors to meld together more fully.
5. **Serve:** Taste the salad and adjust the seasoning with more salt, pepper, or lime juice if needed. Serve chilled or at room temperature.

Kale Caesar Salad (Vegan)

 4 servings    30 minutes

INGREDIENTS

For the Salad:

- 1 large bunch of kale, stems removed and leaves torn into bite-sized pieces
- 1 tablespoon olive oil
- Pinch of salt

For the Vegan Caesar Dressing:

- 1/2 cup raw cashews, soaked for 4 hours or overnight, then drained
- 1/4 cup water (more as needed to reach desired consistency)
- 2 tablespoons lemon juice
- 1 tablespoon olive oil
- 1 tablespoon capers, with a bit of their brine
- 1 teaspoon Dijon mustard
- 1 garlic clove
- 2 teaspoons nutritional yeast
- Salt and black pepper, to taste

For the Croutons:

- 2 cups cubed bread (preferably whole grain or sourdough)
- 2 tablespoons olive oil
- 1/2 teaspoon garlic powder
- Salt and pepper, to taste

DIRECTIONS

1. **Prep the Kale:** Place the torn kale leaves in a large bowl. Drizzle with 1 tablespoon olive oil and a pinch of salt. Massage the kale with your hands for about 3 minutes, or until the leaves are tender and slightly wilted.
2. **Make the Vegan Caesar Dressing:** In a blender, combine the soaked and drained cashews, water, lemon juice, olive oil, capers and brine, Dijon mustard, garlic, nutritional yeast, salt, and pepper. Blend until smooth and creamy. Adjust the seasoning to taste, and add more water if a thinner consistency is desired.
3. **Prepare the Croutons:** Preheat your oven to 375°F (190°C). Toss the cubed bread with olive oil, garlic powder, salt, and pepper until well coated. Spread the cubes on a baking sheet in a single layer. Bake for about 10-15 minutes, or until golden and crispy, stirring halfway through.
4. **Assemble the Salad:** Add the creamy vegan Caesar dressing to the massaged kale leaves, tossing well to coat each leaf evenly. Add the croutons and toss gently to combine.
5. **Serve:** Divide the salad among plates or bowls. If desired, garnish with additional nutritional yeast, black pepper, or vegan parmesan cheese. Serve immediately.

Roasted Beet and Orange Salad

🍴 4 servings 🕐 45 minutes

INGREDIENTS

For the Salad:

- 4 medium beets, peeled and cut into wedges
- 2 tablespoons olive oil
- Salt and pepper, to taste
- 2 large oranges
- 1/4 red onion, thinly sliced
- 1/2 cup walnuts or pecans, toasted and roughly chopped
- A handful of fresh parsley, chopped
- 1/4 cup crumbled vegan feta or goat cheese (optional, for serving)

For the Dressing:

- 3 tablespoons olive oil
- 1 tablespoon white wine vinegar
- 1 tablespoon orange juice (freshly squeezed from the orange)
- 1 teaspoon Dijon mustard
- 1 teaspoon maple syrup or honey (if not strictly vegan)
- Salt and pepper, to taste

DIRECTIONS

1. **Roast the Beets:** Preheat your oven to 400°F (200°C). Toss the beet wedges with 2 tablespoons of olive oil, salt, and pepper. Spread them out on a baking sheet lined with parchment paper. Roast in the preheated oven for about 25-30 minutes, or until tender and slightly caramelized. Allow to cool slightly.

2. **Prepare the Oranges:** While the beets are roasting, peel the oranges. Over a bowl, segment the oranges by cutting between the membranes to release the segments, capturing any juice that falls. Set the segments aside and reserve the juice for the dressing.

3. **Make the Dressing:** In a small bowl, whisk together the dressing ingredients: olive oil, white wine vinegar, 1 tablespoon of the reserved orange juice, Dijon mustard, maple syrup, salt, and pepper. Adjust the seasoning as needed.

4. **Assemble the Salad:** In a large serving bowl, combine the roasted beet wedges, orange segments, and thinly sliced red onion. Drizzle with the prepared dressing and gently toss to combine.

5. **Garnish and Serve:** Top the salad with toasted walnuts or pecans, fresh parsley, and crumbled vegan feta or goat cheese (if using). Serve immediately.

Spinach and Strawberry Salad

🍴 4 servings 🕐 15 minutes

INGREDIENTS

For the Salad:

- 5 cups fresh baby spinach, washed and dried
- 2 cups fresh strawberries, hulled and sliced
- 1/2 cup walnut halves, toasted
- 1/4 red onion, thinly sliced
- 1/2 cup crumbled vegan feta or goat cheese (optional, for a dairy-free version, omit or use a vegan cheese alternative)

For the Balsamic Vinaigrette:

- 1/4 cup extra virgin olive oil
- 2 tablespoons balsamic vinegar
- 1 tablespoon maple syrup or agave nectar
- 1 teaspoon Dijon mustard
- Salt and pepper, to taste

DIRECTIONS

1. **Prepare the Vinaigrette:** In a small bowl or jar, whisk together the olive oil, balsamic vinegar, maple syrup, Dijon mustard, salt, and pepper. Adjust the seasonings to taste. Set aside to let the flavors meld.
2. **Assemble the Salad:** In a large salad bowl, combine the baby spinach, sliced strawberries, toasted walnuts, and thinly sliced red onion. If using, sprinkle the crumbled vegan feta or goat cheese over the top.
3. **Dress the Salad:** Drizzle the balsamic vinaigrette over the salad just before serving. Gently toss to ensure all the ingredients are evenly coated with the dressing.
4. **Serve:** Divide the salad among plates or bowls and serve immediately. This salad is best enjoyed fresh.

Carrot and Cabbage Slaw

 4-6 servings  15 minutes

INGREDIENTS

For the Slaw:

- 4 cups green cabbage, thinly sliced
- 2 cups red cabbage, thinly sliced (for color contrast)
- 2 large carrots, peeled and julienned or grated
- 1/2 red onion, thinly sliced
- 1/4 cup fresh parsley, chopped

For the Vinaigrette:

- 1/4 cup apple cider vinegar
- 2 tablespoons olive oil
- 1 tablespoon Dijon mustard
- 1 tablespoon maple syrup or honey (use maple syrup to keep it vegan)
- Salt and pepper, to taste

DIRECTIONS

1. **Prepare the Vegetables:** In a large mixing bowl, combine the thinly sliced green and red cabbage, julienned or grated carrots, thinly sliced red onion, and chopped parsley. Toss until well mixed.
2. **Make the Vinaigrette:** In a small bowl or jar, whisk together the apple cider vinegar, olive oil, Dijon mustard, maple syrup (or honey), salt, and pepper. Taste and adjust the seasoning as needed.
3. **Dress the Slaw:** Pour the vinaigrette over the slaw mixture and toss until all the vegetables are evenly coated. For the best flavor, let the slaw sit for at least 30 minutes in the refrigerator before serving. This resting time allows the flavors to meld and the vegetables to slightly soften, absorbing the dressing.
4. **Serve:** Give the slaw a final toss before serving. Check for seasoning and adjust if necessary. Serve chilled or at room temperature.

Vegan Greek Salad

 4 servings　 15 minutes

INGREDIENTS

For the Salad:

- 1 large cucumber, diced
- 4 medium tomatoes, cut into wedges
- 1 red onion, thinly sliced
- 1 bell pepper (red or green), sliced
- 1 cup Kalamata olives, pitted
- 1 cup vegan feta cheese, crumbled (look for a brand that suits your taste or use a homemade tofu feta)
- 1/4 cup fresh parsley, chopped

For the Dressing:

- 1/4 cup extra virgin olive oil
- 2 tablespoons red wine vinegar
- 1 teaspoon Dijon mustard
- 1 clove garlic, minced
- 1/2 teaspoon dried oregano
- Salt and pepper, to taste

DIRECTIONS

1. **Prepare the Vegetables:** In a large bowl, combine the diced cucumber, tomato wedges, thinly sliced red onion, sliced bell pepper, and Kalamata olives. Toss gently to mix.
2. **Make the Dressing:** In a small bowl or jar, whisk together the extra virgin olive oil, red wine vinegar, Dijon mustard, minced garlic, dried oregano, salt, and pepper until well combined. Taste and adjust seasoning as needed.
3. **Dress the Salad:** Pour the dressing over the salad and toss gently to ensure all the ingredients are evenly coated.
4. **Add Vegan Feta and Parsley:** Sprinkle the crumbled vegan feta cheese and chopped parsley over the top of the salad. Give it a final gentle toss.
5. **Serve:** The salad can be served immediately or chilled for a bit in the refrigerator to let the flavors meld together. It's best enjoyed fresh, but leftovers can be stored in the refrigerator for up to 2 days.

Warm Lentil and Potato Salad

 4 servings  45 minutes

INGREDIENTS

For the Salad:

- 1 cup green or brown lentils, rinsed
- 2 cups vegetable broth or water
- 1 bay leaf (optional)
- 1 lb (about 450g) small potatoes, halved or quartered depending on size
- 1 tablespoon olive oil
- Salt and pepper, to taste
- 1 small red onion, finely diced
- 2 tablespoons capers, rinsed and drained
- 1/4 cup fresh parsley, chopped

For the Mustard Dressing:

- 3 tablespoons olive oil
- 2 tablespoons apple cider vinegar
- 1 tablespoon Dijon mustard
- 1 garlic clove, minced
- Salt and pepper, to taste

DIRECTIONS

1. **Cook the Lentils:** In a medium saucepan, combine the lentils, vegetable broth (or water), and a bay leaf. Bring to a boil, then reduce heat and simmer, covered, for 20-25 minutes, or until the lentils are tender but still hold their shape. Drain any excess liquid and remove the bay leaf.
2. **Roast the Potatoes:** Preheat your oven to 425°F (220°C). Toss the potatoes with 1 tablespoon of olive oil, salt, and pepper. Spread them in a single layer on a baking sheet. Roast for 20-25 minutes, or until golden and tender, stirring halfway through.
3. **Prepare the Dressing:** While the lentils and potatoes are cooking, whisk together the olive oil, apple cider vinegar, Dijon mustard, minced garlic, salt, and pepper in a small bowl. Set aside.
4. **Combine the Salad:** In a large bowl, combine the warm lentils, roasted potatoes, red onion, capers, and parsley. Pour the mustard dressing over the salad and toss gently to combine. Taste and adjust the seasoning as needed.
5. **Serve:** Enjoy the salad warm, garnished with additional parsley if desired.

Arugula, Pear, and Walnut Salad

4 servings · 15 minutes

INGREDIENTS

For the Salad:

- 5 cups arugula, washed and dried
- 2 ripe pears, cored and thinly sliced
- 1/2 cup walnuts, toasted and roughly chopped
- 1/2 cup vegan feta cheese, crumbled (optional)

For the Vinaigrette:

- 1/4 cup extra virgin olive oil
- 2 tablespoons balsamic vinegar
- 1 teaspoon Dijon mustard
- 1 teaspoon maple syrup or agave nectar
- Salt and black pepper, to taste

DIRECTIONS

1. **Prepare the Vinaigrette:** In a small bowl or jar, whisk together the olive oil, balsamic vinegar, Dijon mustard, maple syrup, salt, and pepper until well combined. Adjust the seasoning to your taste. Set aside.
2. **Toast the Walnuts:** Preheat a small pan over medium heat. Add the walnuts and toast them, stirring occasionally, for about 5-7 minutes or until they become fragrant and slightly darker in color. Be careful not to burn them. Remove from heat and let cool.
3. **Assemble the Salad:** In a large salad bowl, combine the arugula, sliced pears, and toasted walnuts. If using, add the crumbled vegan feta cheese to the bowl.
4. **Dress the Salad:** Drizzle the vinaigrette over the salad just before serving. Gently toss everything together to ensure the salad ingredients are evenly coated with the dressing.
5. **Serve:** Divide the salad among plates. Serve immediately as a refreshing starter, a light meal, or a side dish to your main course.

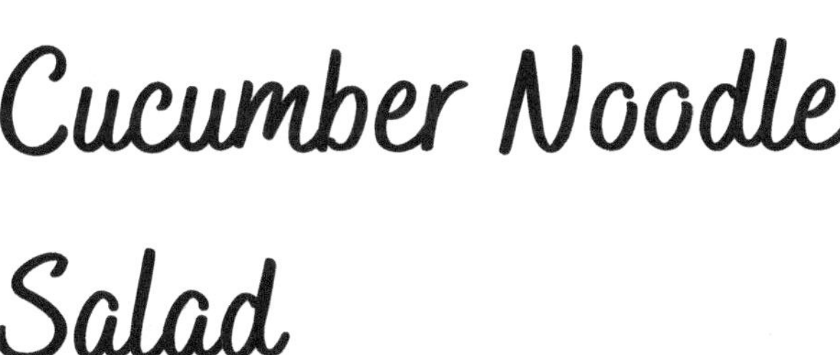

Cucumber Noodle Salad

🍴 4 servings   🕐 20 minutes

INGREDIENTS

For the Salad:

- 2 large cucumbers
- 1 carrot, julienned or spiralized (optional, for color and texture)
- 1/4 red onion, thinly sliced
- 1/4 cup chopped fresh herbs (such as mint, cilantro, or basil)

For the Dressing:

- 3 tablespoons rice vinegar
- 1 tablespoon sesame oil
- 1 tablespoon soy sauce or tamari (for gluten-free option)
- 1 teaspoon maple syrup or honey
- 1 clove garlic, minced
- 1 teaspoon grated fresh ginger
- Salt and pepper, to taste
- Optional: A pinch of red pepper flakes for heat

Optional Toppings:

- Sesame seeds
- Crushed peanuts or cashews
- Lime wedges for serving

DIRECTIONS

1. **Prepare the Cucumber Noodles:** Use a spiralizer to turn the cucumbers into noodles. If you don't have a spiralizer, you can use a vegetable peeler to create thin ribbons. Place the cucumber noodles in a colander, sprinkle with a little salt, and let them sit for about 10 minutes to draw out excess water. Gently press to remove moisture, then transfer to a large salad bowl.
2. **Mix the Salad Ingredients:** Add the julienned carrot, thinly sliced red onion, and chopped herbs to the bowl with the cucumber noodles. Toss gently to combine.
3. **Make the Dressing:** In a small bowl, whisk together the rice vinegar, sesame oil, soy sauce, maple syrup, minced garlic, grated ginger, salt, pepper, and red pepper flakes (if using) until well combined.
4. **Dress the Salad:** Pour the dressing over the cucumber noodle mixture and toss gently until everything is evenly coated.
5. **Serve:** Garnish the salad with sesame seeds and crushed peanuts or cashews if using. Serve with lime wedges on the side.

Roasted Squash and Pomegranate Salad

 4 servings    45 minutes

INGREDIENTS

For the Salad:

- 1 medium butternut squash (about 2 lbs), peeled, seeded, and cut into 1-inch cubes
- 2 tablespoons olive oil
- Salt and pepper, to taste
- 1 cup pomegranate seeds
- 4 cups mixed greens (such as arugula, spinach, or kale)
- 1/2 cup toasted walnuts, roughly chopped
- 1/2 cup crumbled vegan feta cheese (optional)

For the Dressing:

- 3 tablespoons olive oil
- 1 tablespoon balsamic vinegar
- 1 tablespoon maple syrup
- 1 teaspoon Dijon mustard
- Salt and pepper, to taste

DIRECTIONS

1. **Roast the Squash**: Preheat your oven to 400°F (200°C). Toss the butternut squash cubes with 2 tablespoons of olive oil, salt, and pepper on a baking sheet. Spread them out in a single layer. Roast in the oven for 25-30 minutes, turning once, until the squash is tender and caramelized on the edges. Let it cool slightly.
2. **Prepare the Dressing**: In a small bowl, whisk together the olive oil, balsamic vinegar, maple syrup, and Dijon mustard. Season with salt and pepper to taste. Adjust the seasoning and sweetness according to your preference.
3. **Assemble the Salad**: In a large bowl, combine the roasted squash, pomegranate seeds, mixed greens, toasted walnuts, and crumbled vegan feta cheese (if using).
4. **Toss with Dressing**: Drizzle the dressing over the salad and gently toss to combine, making sure the squash and greens are well coated.
5. **Serve**: Serve the salad immediately, or let it sit for about 10 minutes to allow the flavors to meld together.

Crispy Tofu and Mango Salad

 4 servings    30 minutes

INGREDIENTS

For the salad:

- 1 block (14 oz) firm tofu, pressed and cut into cubes
- 2 tablespoons cornstarch
- Salt and pepper, to taste
- 2 tablespoons olive oil or vegetable oil, for frying
- 2 ripe mangoes, peeled and sliced into strips
- 4 cups mixed salad greens (like baby spinach, arugula, or mixed lettuce)
- 1 small red onion, thinly sliced
- 1/4 cup fresh cilantro, chopped
- 1/4 cup roasted peanuts or cashews, for garnish

For the Dressing:

- 3 tablespoons lime juice
- 2 tablespoons soy sauce or tamari
- 1 tablespoon sesame oil
- 1 tablespoon maple syrup or honey
- 1 garlic clove, minced
- 1 teaspoon grated ginger

DIRECTIONS

1. **Prepare the Tofu:** Toss the cubed tofu with cornstarch, salt, and pepper, ensuring each piece is evenly coated. Heat oil in a large pan over medium-high heat. Add the tofu and fry until golden and crispy on all sides. Transfer to a paper towel-lined plate to drain any excess oil.

2. **Make the Dressing:** In a small bowl, whisk together lime juice, soy sauce, sesame oil, maple syrup, garlic, and ginger until well combined. Adjust the seasoning as needed.

3. **Assemble the Salad:** In a large bowl, combine the mixed salad greens, sliced mango, red onion, and cilantro. Add the crispy tofu on top.

4. **Dress the Salad:** Drizzle the dressing over the salad and gently toss to ensure everything is evenly coated.

5. **Serve:** Garnish with roasted peanuts or cashews right before serving.

Vegan Waldorf Salad

 4 servings　　 45 minutes

INGREDIENTS

For the salad:

- 2 large apples (preferably a crisp variety like Granny Smith or Honeycrisp), cored and chopped into bite-sized pieces
- 1 cup red seedless grapes, halved
- 1 cup celery, thinly sliced
- 1/2 cup walnuts, roughly chopped (toasted for extra flavor, optional)
- 1/2 cup raisins or dried cranberries (optional for added sweetness and texture)

For the Vegan Dressing:

- 1/2 cup vegan mayonnaise
- 2 tablespoons lemon juice
- 1 tablespoon maple syrup or agave nectar
- Salt and pepper, to taste

DIRECTIONS

1. **Prepare the Salad Components:** In a large bowl, combine the chopped apples, halved grapes, sliced celery, chopped walnuts, and raisins or dried cranberries if using. Toss lightly to mix.
2. **Make the Dressing:** In a small bowl, whisk together the vegan mayonnaise, lemon juice, and maple syrup until smooth. Season with salt and pepper to your taste.
3. **Dress the Salad:** Pour the dressing over the salad ingredients in the large bowl. Gently toss until all the components are evenly coated with the dressing.
4. **Chill Before Serving:** For the best flavor, let the salad chill in the refrigerator for at least 30 minutes before serving. This allows the flavors to meld together.
5. **Serve:** Transfer the salad to a serving dish or individual plates. Optionally, garnish with additional chopped walnuts or a sprinkle of paprika for color.

Edamame and Quinoa Salad with Ginger Dressing

☆☆☆☆☆

 4 servings  35 minutes

INGREDIENTS

For the Salad:

- 1 cup quinoa, rinsed
- 2 cups water
- 1 cup edamame, shelled and cooked
- 1 red bell pepper, diced
- 1 carrot, julienned or shredded
- 1/4 cup red cabbage, thinly sliced
- 1/4 cup fresh cilantro, chopped
- 2 green onions, thinly sliced
- 1/4 cup toasted sesame seeds or slivered almonds (for garnish)

For the Ginger Dressing:

- 1/4 cup olive oil
- 2 tablespoons rice vinegar
- 1 tablespoon fresh ginger, grated
- 1 clove garlic, minced
- 1 tablespoon soy sauce or tamari
- 1 teaspoon maple syrup or agave nectar
- Salt and pepper, to taste

DIRECTIONS

1. **Cook the Quinoa:** In a medium saucepan, bring 2 cups of water to a boil. Add the rinsed quinoa, reduce heat to low, cover, and simmer for 15 minutes or until the water is absorbed and the quinoa is fluffy. Remove from heat and let it cool.

2. **Prepare the Dressing:** In a small bowl, whisk together olive oil, rice vinegar, grated ginger, minced garlic, soy sauce, and maple syrup until well combined. Season with salt and pepper to taste.

3. **Assemble the Salad:** In a large bowl, combine the cooled quinoa, cooked edamame, diced red bell pepper, julienned carrot, sliced red cabbage, chopped cilantro, and sliced green onions.

4. **Dress the Salad:** Pour the ginger dressing over the salad and toss gently to ensure everything is evenly coated.

5. **Garnish and Serve:** Sprinkle toasted sesame seeds or slivered almonds over the top for added crunch and flavor. Serve the salad at room temperature or chilled, according to your preference.

Vegan Caesar Salad with Crispy Chickpeas

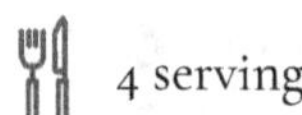

4 servings   40 minutes

INGREDIENTS

For the Salad:

- 2 heads of romaine lettuce, washed and chopped
- 1 cup cherry tomatoes, halved
- 1 avocado, sliced (optional)

For the Crispy Chickpeas:

- 1 can (15 oz) chickpeas, drained, rinsed, and dried
- 1 tablespoon olive oil
- 1/2 teaspoon garlic powder
- Salt and pepper, to taste

For the Vegan Caesar Dressing:

- 1/2 cup raw cashews, soaked for 4 hours or overnight, then drained
- 1/4 cup water
- 2 tablespoons lemon juice
- 1 tablespoon olive oil
- 1 teaspoon Dijon mustard
- 2 cloves garlic
- 2 teaspoons capers
- 1 tablespoon nutritional yeast
- Salt and pepper, to taste

For the Vegan Parmesan:

- 1/2 cup raw cashews
- 2 tablespoons nutritional yeast
- 1/2 teaspoon garlic powder
- Salt, to taste

DIRECTIONS

1. **Prepare the Crispy Chickpeas:** Preheat your oven to 400°F (200°C). Toss the chickpeas with olive oil, garlic powder, salt, and pepper. Spread them on a baking sheet and roast for 20-25 minutes until crispy. Set aside to cool.

2. **Make the Vegan Caesar Dressing:** In a blender, combine the soaked and drained cashews, water, lemon juice, olive oil, Dijon mustard, garlic, capers, and nutritional yeast. Blend until smooth and creamy. Season with salt and pepper to taste. Adjust the thickness by adding a bit more water if necessary.

3. **Prepare the Vegan Parmesan:** In a food processor, pulse the cashews, nutritional yeast, garlic powder, and salt until the mixture resembles fine crumbs. Be careful not to over-process into a paste.

4. **Assemble the Salad:** In a large bowl, toss the chopped romaine lettuce with the vegan Caesar dressing until well coated. Add the cherry tomatoes and avocado slices if using.

5. **Serve:** Top the salad with crispy chickpeas and a generous sprinkle of vegan Parmesan. Serve immediately.

Spicy Peanut and Cucumber Salad

🍴 4 servings   🕐 15 minutes

INGREDIENTS

For the Salad:

- 2 large cucumbers, thinly sliced
- 1 red bell pepper, thinly sliced
- 1 carrot, julienned
- 1/4 red onion, thinly sliced
- 1/4 cup fresh cilantro, chopped
- 1/4 cup roasted peanuts, for garnish

For the Spicy Peanut Dressing:

- 1/4 cup smooth peanut butter
- 2 tablespoons soy sauce or tamari
- 1 tablespoon rice vinegar
- 1 tablespoon maple syrup or honey
- 1–2 teaspoons chili garlic sauce or Sriracha (adjust to taste)
- 1 clove garlic, minced
- 1 teaspoon grated fresh ginger
- 2–3 tablespoons warm water (to thin the dressing)

DIRECTIONS

1. **Prepare the Salad:** In a large bowl, combine the thinly sliced cucumbers, red bell pepper, julienned carrot, thinly sliced red onion, and chopped cilantro.

2. **Make the Spicy Peanut Dressing:** In a small bowl, whisk together the peanut butter, soy sauce, rice vinegar, maple syrup, chili garlic sauce, minced garlic, and grated ginger. Gradually add warm water one tablespoon at a time until the dressing reaches your desired consistency. It should be creamy but pourable.

3. **Dress the Salad:** Pour the spicy peanut dressing over the salad ingredients in the bowl. Toss gently until all the vegetables are evenly coated with the dressing.

4. **Garnish and Serve:** Sprinkle roasted peanuts over the top of the salad for an added crunch. Serve immediately, or chill in the refrigerator for 30 minutes to allow the flavors to meld together before serving.

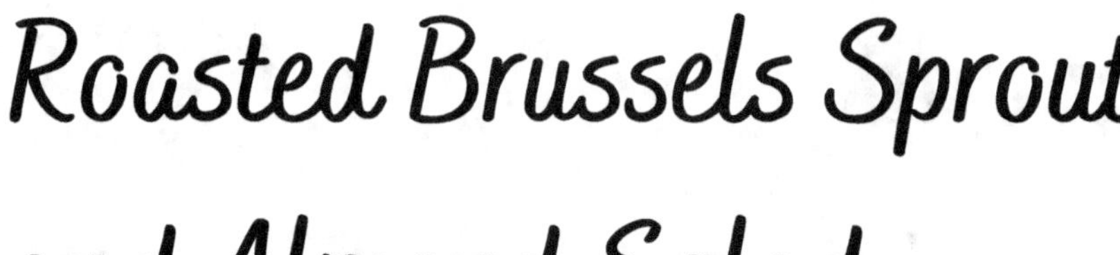

Roasted Brussels Sprouts and Almond Salad

 4 servings    35 minutes

INGREDIENTS

For the Salad:

- 1 lb Brussels sprouts, trimmed and halved
- 2 tablespoons olive oil
- Salt and pepper, to taste
- 1/2 cup whole almonds (you can use sliced or slivered almonds if preferred)
- 1/4 cup dried cranberries or cherries for a touch of sweetness (optional)
- 2 cups mixed salad greens or baby spinach

For the Dressing:

- 3 tablespoons olive oil
- 1 tablespoon apple cider vinegar
- 1 tablespoon maple syrup or honey
- 1 teaspoon Dijon mustard
- Salt and pepper, to taste

DIRECTIONS

1. **Roast the Brussels Sprouts:** Preheat your oven to 400°F (200°C). Toss the Brussels sprouts with 2 tablespoons of olive oil, salt, and pepper. Spread them on a baking sheet in a single layer. Roast in the oven for 20-25 minutes or until they are golden and crispy on the outside and tender on the inside. Let them cool slightly.
2. **Toast the Almonds:** While the Brussels sprouts are roasting, toast the almonds in a dry skillet over medium heat, stirring frequently, until they are golden and fragrant. Be careful not to burn them. Set aside to cool.
3. **Prepare the Dressing:** In a small bowl, whisk together the olive oil, apple cider vinegar, maple syrup, Dijon mustard, salt, and pepper until well combined and emulsified.
4. **Assemble the Salad:** In a large salad bowl, combine the roasted Brussels sprouts, toasted almonds, dried cranberries (if using), and mixed greens. Drizzle the dressing over the salad and toss gently to ensure everything is evenly coated.
5. **Serve:** Serve the salad warm or at room temperature.

Vegan Cobb Salad with Coconut Bacon

 4 servings    35 minutes

INGREDIENTS

For the Salad:

- 6 cups mixed salad greens (such as romaine, baby spinach, and arugula)
- 1 cup cherry tomatoes, halved
- 1 ripe avocado, diced
- 1 cup cooked and cooled quinoa
- 1 can (15 oz) chickpeas, drained, rinsed, and dried
- 1 small red onion, thinly sliced
- 1/2 cup shredded carrots
- 1/2 cup corn kernels (fresh, canned, or thawed if frozen)

For the Coconut Bacon:

- 1 cup unsweetened coconut flakes
- 1 tablespoon soy sauce or tamari
- 1 tablespoon maple syrup
- 1/2 teaspoon smoked paprika

For the Dressing:

- 1/4 cup olive oil
- 2 tablespoons apple cider vinegar
- 1 tablespoon Dijon mustard
- 1 tablespoon maple syrup or agave nectar
- Salt and pepper, to taste

DIRECTIONS

1. **Prepare the Coconut Bacon:** Preheat your oven to 325°F (165°C). In a bowl, mix the coconut flakes with soy sauce, maple syrup, and smoked paprika until well coated. Spread the coconut flakes on a baking sheet lined with parchment paper in a single layer. Bake for 10-15 minutes, stirring occasionally, until crisp and browned. Watch closely to prevent burning. Let cool.
2. **Assemble the Salad:** In a large serving bowl, arrange the mixed greens as a base. Create neat rows of cherry tomatoes, diced avocado, cooked quinoa, chickpeas, red onion, shredded carrots, and corn over the greens.
3. **Make the Dressing:** In a small bowl, whisk together olive oil, apple cider vinegar, Dijon mustard, maple syrup, salt, and pepper until emulsified.
4. **Serve:** Sprinkle the cooled coconut bacon over the salad. Drizzle the dressing over the salad just before serving, or serve it on the side for individuals to add as they like.

Watermelon and Avocado Salad

🍴 4 servings   🕐 15 minutes

INGREDIENTS

For the Salad:

- 4 cups watermelon, cubed
- 2 ripe avocados, pitted, peeled, and cubed
- 1/2 cup cucumber, thinly sliced
- 1/4 cup red onion, thinly sliced
- 1/4 cup fresh mint leaves, roughly chopped
- 1/4 cup feta cheese, crumbled (use vegan feta to keep it plant-based)

For the Dressing:

- 3 tablespoons olive oil
- 2 tablespoons lime juice
- 1 teaspoon maple syrup or agave nectar
- Salt and pepper, to taste
- Optional: a pinch of chili flakes for a bit of heat

DIRECTIONS

1. **Prepare the Salad Ingredients:** In a large bowl, gently combine the cubed watermelon, cubed avocados, sliced cucumber, sliced red onion, and chopped mint. Handle the avocados gently to keep them from mashing into the salad.
2. **Whisk Together the Dressing:** In a small bowl, whisk together olive oil, lime juice, maple syrup, salt, pepper, and chili flakes (if using) until well combined.
3. **Dress the Salad:** Drizzle the dressing over the salad just before serving. Gently toss to ensure all ingredients are lightly coated.
4. **Serve:** Sprinkle crumbled feta cheese over the top of the salad. Serve immediately to enjoy the freshness of the ingredients.

# Kale and Apple Salad with Lemon Vinaigrette

4 servings   20 minutes

INGREDIENTS

For the Salad:

- 6 cups kale, stems removed and leaves thinly sliced
- 2 medium apples (such as Granny Smith or Fuji), cored and thinly sliced
- 1/2 cup walnuts, toasted and roughly chopped
- 1/4 cup dried cranberries or raisins
- 1/4 cup grated Parmesan cheese (use vegan Parmesan to keep it plant-based)

For the Lemon Vinaigrette:

- 1/4 cup extra virgin olive oil
- 2 tablespoons fresh lemon juice
- 1 tablespoon apple cider vinegar
- 1 teaspoon Dijon mustard
- 1 teaspoon maple syrup or honey
- Salt and pepper, to taste

DIRECTIONS

1. **Massage the Kale:** Place the thinly sliced kale in a large bowl. Add a small drizzle of olive oil and a pinch of salt. Using your hands, massage the kale for 2–3 minutes until it starts to soften and wilt. This process makes the kale more tender and easier to digest.
2. **Prepare the Lemon Vinaigrette:** In a small bowl or jar, whisk or shake together the olive oil, lemon juice, apple cider vinegar, Dijon mustard, maple syrup, salt, and pepper until well combined and emulsified.
3. **Assemble the Salad:** To the bowl of massaged kale, add the thinly sliced apples, toasted walnuts, dried cranberries, and grated Parmesan cheese.
4. **Dress the Salad:** Drizzle the lemon vinaigrette over the salad and toss gently to ensure everything is evenly coated.
5. **Serve:** Serve the salad immediately, or let it sit for about 10 minutes to allow the flavors to meld together.

Snacks and Sides

Hummus with Vegetable Sticks

 4-6 servings    15 minutes

INGREDIENTS

For the Hummus:

- 1 can (15 oz) chickpeas, drained and rinsed
- 1/4 cup tahini (sesame seed paste)
- 2 tablespoons olive oil
- Juice of 1 lemon
- 1-2 cloves garlic, minced
- 1/2 teaspoon ground cumin
- Salt to taste
- 2-4 tablespoons water (as needed for consistency)
- Paprika and additional olive oil for garnish

For the Vegetable Sticks:

- Carrots, peeled and cut into sticks
- Cucumbers, sliced into sticks
- Bell peppers (red, yellow, or green), cut into strips
- Celery, cut into sticks
- Any other vegetables of your choice

DIRECTIONS

1. **Make the Hummus:** In a food processor, combine the chickpeas, tahini, olive oil, lemon juice, minced garlic, cumin, and a pinch of salt. Blend until smooth. Gradually add water, 1 tablespoon at a time, until you reach your desired consistency. Taste and adjust the seasoning as needed.
2. **Prepare the Vegetables:** While the hummus is blending, wash and prepare your vegetables. Cut them into sticks or strips that are easy to dip.
3. **Serve:** Transfer the hummus to a serving bowl. Create a small well in the center of the hummus and pour in a little olive oil. Sprinkle paprika over the top for color and added flavor. Arrange the vegetable sticks around the hummus or on a separate platter for serving.
4. **Enjoy:** Dip the vegetable sticks into the hummus and enjoy!

Stuffed Bell Peppers

 4 servings    1 hour

INGREDIENTS

For the Stuffed Peppers:

- 4 large bell peppers, any color
- 1 cup quinoa, rinsed
- 2 cups vegetable broth
- 1 tablespoon olive oil
- 1 small onion, diced
- 2 cloves garlic, minced
- 1 zucchini, diced
- 1 cup black beans, drained and rinsed
- 1 cup corn kernels (fresh, frozen, or canned)
- 1 teaspoon ground cumin
- 1 teaspoon chili powder
- 1/2 teaspoon smoked paprika
- Salt and pepper, to taste
- 1 cup tomato sauce
- 1/2 cup vegan cheese shreds (optional)

For Garnish (Optional):

- Fresh cilantro, chopped
- Avocado slices
- Lime wedges
- Vegan sour cream

DIRECTIONS

1. **Prep the Peppers:** Preheat your oven to 375°F (190°C). Slice the tops off the bell peppers and remove the seeds and membranes. If necessary, slice a tiny bit off the bottom of each pepper so they stand up straight. Set aside.

2. **Cook the Quinoa:** In a saucepan, bring the vegetable broth to a boil. Add the quinoa, reduce heat to low, cover, and simmer for about 15 minutes, or until the liquid is absorbed and the quinoa is tender. Remove from heat and let it sit, covered, for 5 minutes. Fluff with a fork.

3. **Sauté the Vegetables:** While the quinoa is cooking, heat the olive oil in a large skillet over medium heat. Add the onion and garlic, sautéing until soft and fragrant, about 3-4 minutes. Add the zucchini, black beans, corn, cumin, chili powder, smoked paprika, salt, and pepper. Cook for another 5 minutes, stirring occasionally.

4. **Combine:** Mix the cooked quinoa into the skillet with the vegetable mixture. Stir in half of the tomato sauce, adjusting seasoning as needed.

5. **Stuff the Peppers:** Spoon the quinoa and vegetable mixture into each bell pepper, packing it tightly. Place the stuffed peppers in a baking dish. Pour the remaining tomato sauce over the peppers. Cover the dish with foil.

6. **Bake:** Bake in the preheated oven for about 30-35 minutes. Uncover, sprinkle vegan cheese on top of each pepper (if using), and bake for an additional 10 minutes, or until the cheese is melted and the peppers are tender.

7. **Serve:** Let the stuffed peppers cool for a few minutes before serving. Garnish with chopped cilantro, avocado slices, lime wedges, and a dollop of vegan sour cream, if desired.

Vegan Spring Rolls

🍴 8-10 servings   🕐 30 minutes

INGREDIENTS

For the Spring Rolls:

- 8-10 rice paper wrappers
- 1 cup purple cabbage, thinly sliced
- 1 large carrot, julienned or grated
- 1 cucumber, julienned
- 1 bell pepper (any color), julienned
- 1 avocado, sliced
- 1 cup fresh lettuce leaves or baby spinach
- 1/2 cup fresh herbs (mint, basil, cilantro), leaves picked
- 1 block (14 oz) firm tofu, pressed and cut into thin strips (optional)
- Cooked rice noodles or vermicelli (optional)

For the Peanut Dipping Sauce:

- 1/4 cup peanut butter
- 2 tablespoons soy sauce or tamari (for gluten-free)
- 1 tablespoon maple syrup or agave nectar
- 1 tablespoon lime juice
- 1 clove garlic, minced
- 1 teaspoon grated ginger
- Water to thin, as needed
- Optional: Chili flakes or hot sauce for heat

DIRECTIONS

1. **Prepare the Fillings:** Prep all your vegetables, herbs, and tofu (if using) and set them aside in separate bowls or on a large platter for easy assembly.
2. **Soften the Rice Paper:** Fill a large dish or pie plate with warm water. Dip one rice paper wrapper into the water for about 10-15 seconds or until it becomes pliable but not too soft. Lay the wrapper flat on a clean, slightly damp kitchen towel.
3. **Assemble the Spring Rolls:** On the bottom third of the wrapper, place a small amount of lettuce or spinach, a few pieces of each vegetable, a few herb leaves, and a couple of tofu strips or some noodles (if using). Don't overfill to ensure easy rolling.
4. **Roll Them Up:** Fold the bottom of the wrapper tightly over the filling, then fold in the sides and continue to roll up tightly until sealed. Place the finished roll on a plate and cover with a damp cloth to keep it moist. Repeat with the remaining wrappers and fillings.
5. **Make the Peanut Dipping Sauce:** In a small bowl, whisk together the peanut butter, soy sauce, maple syrup, lime juice, garlic, ginger, and enough water to reach your desired consistency. Add chili flakes or hot sauce if you like it spicy.
6. **Serve:** Cut the spring rolls in half diagonally (optional) and serve with the peanut dipping sauce.

Garlic and Herb Roasted Potatoes

 4-6 servings  40 minutes

INGREDIENTS

- 2 pounds (about 900g) small potatoes (Yukon Gold, red, or baby potatoes work well), halved or quartered depending on size
- 1/4 cup olive oil
- 3-4 cloves garlic, minced
- 1 tablespoon fresh rosemary, finely chopped
- 1 tablespoon fresh thyme, finely chopped
- Salt and pepper, to taste
- Optional: 1 teaspoon paprika for color and a slight smoky flavor

DIRECTIONS

1. **Preheat the Oven:** Preheat your oven to 425°F (220°C). Line a baking sheet with parchment paper for easy cleanup.
2. **Prepare the Potatoes:** Wash the potatoes thoroughly and cut them into halves or quarters, ensuring they are about the same size for even cooking.
3. **Season:** In a large bowl, combine the olive oil, minced garlic, chopped rosemary, chopped thyme, salt, pepper, and paprika (if using). Add the potatoes to the bowl and toss until they are well coated with the seasoning mixture.
4. **Arrange on Baking Sheet:** Spread the potatoes out in a single layer on the prepared baking sheet. Make sure they aren't overcrowded to ensure they roast properly and get crispy.
5. **Roast:** Place the baking sheet in the preheated oven and roast the potatoes for about 25-30 minutes, or until they are golden brown and crispy on the outside and tender on the inside. Halfway through the cooking time, use a spatula to flip the potatoes to ensure even browning.
6. **Serve:** Once the potatoes are roasted to your liking, remove them from the oven and let them cool slightly on the baking sheet. Taste and adjust the seasoning with additional salt and pepper if necessary. Serve warm as a side dish.

Vegan Nachos with Cashew Cheese

🍴 4-6 servings 🕐 30 minutes

INGREDIENTS

For the Cashew Cheese Sauce:

- 1 cup raw cashews, soaked for 4 hours or overnight, then drained
- 1/2 cup water
- 2 tablespoons nutritional yeast
- 1 tablespoon lemon juice
- 1 teaspoon apple cider vinegar
- 1/2 teaspoon garlic powder
- 1/2 teaspoon onion powder
- Salt to taste
- Optional: a pinch of turmeric for color

For the Nachos:

- 8 oz (about 225g) tortilla chips
- 1 can (15 oz) black beans, rinsed and drained
- 1 large tomato, diced
- 1 avocado, diced
- 1/2 red onion, finely chopped
- 1 jalapeño, thinly sliced (adjust to taste)
- Fresh cilantro, chopped (for garnish)
- Lime wedges (for serving)

Optional Toppings:

- Salsa
- Vegan sour cream
- Sliced olives
- Corn kernels

DIRECTIONS

1. **Make the Cashew Cheese Sauce:** In a blender, combine the soaked and drained cashews, water, nutritional yeast, lemon juice, apple cider vinegar, garlic powder, onion powder, and salt (and turmeric if using). Blend until smooth and creamy. Adjust the consistency by adding a little more water if needed. Taste and adjust the seasoning as needed.

2. **Prepare the Nachos:** Preheat the oven to 375°F (190°C) if you prefer your nachos warm. On a large baking sheet or oven-proof platter, spread out the tortilla chips in an even layer. Drizzle a generous amount of cashew cheese sauce over the chips. Scatter the black beans and any other toppings you like over the top.

3. **Bake (Optional):** For warm nachos, bake in the preheated oven for about 5-7 minutes, or until the nachos are heated through. For room-temperature nachos, skip this step.

4. **Add Fresh Toppings:** Once out of the oven or if serving at room temperature, add the fresh toppings: diced tomato, diced avocado, chopped red onion, sliced jalapeño, and anything else you're using.

5. **Garnish and Serve:** Garnish with chopped fresh cilantro and serve immediately with lime wedges on the side.

Baked Sweet Potato Fries

☆☆☆☆☆

4 servings • 35 minutes

INGREDIENTS

- 2 large sweet potatoes, peeled
- 2 tablespoons olive oil
- 1 teaspoon paprika
- 1/2 teaspoon garlic powder
- 1/2 teaspoon onion powder
- Salt and pepper, to taste
- Optional: Pinch of cayenne pepper for a spicy kick

DIRECTIONS

1. **Preheat the Oven:** Start by preheating your oven to 425°F (220°C). Line a baking sheet with parchment paper for easy cleanup.
2. **Cut the Sweet Potatoes:** Slice the sweet potatoes into 1/4-inch thick sticks, trying to keep them as uniform as possible to ensure even cooking.
3. **Season:** In a large bowl, toss the sweet potato sticks with olive oil, paprika, garlic powder, onion powder, salt, pepper, and cayenne pepper (if using) until they are evenly coated.
4. **Arrange on Baking Sheet:** Spread the sweet potato fries out in a single layer on the prepared baking sheet, making sure they are not touching each other too much. This helps them become crispier.
5. **Bake:** Place the baking sheet in the oven and bake for about 20-25 minutes, or until the fries are golden brown and crispy on the edges. Flip the fries halfway through the baking time to ensure they brown evenly on all sides.
6. **Serve:** Remove the fries from the oven and let them cool for a few minutes on the baking sheet. They will continue to crisp up as they cool. Serve warm with your favorite dipping sauce.

Cauliflower Buffalo Wings

🍴 4 servings 🕐 50 minutes

INGREDIENTS

For the Cauliflower:
- 1 large head of cauliflower, cut into bite-sized florets
- 3/4 cup all-purpose flour (use gluten-free flour if necessary)
- 1 cup water
- 1/2 teaspoon garlic powder
- Salt and pepper, to taste
- 1 cup breadcrumbs (optional, for extra crunch)

For the Buffalo Sauce:
- 1/2 cup hot sauce (such as Frank's RedHot)
- 1/4 cup vegan butter, melted
- 1 tablespoon maple syrup or agave nectar

DIRECTIONS

1. **Preheat the Oven:** Preheat your oven to 450°F (230°C). Line a baking sheet with parchment paper.
2. **Prepare the Batter:** In a large bowl, whisk together the flour, water, garlic powder, salt, and pepper until smooth. If using breadcrumbs for extra crunch, place them in a separate shallow dish.
3. **Coat the Cauliflower:** Dip each cauliflower floret into the batter, making sure it's evenly coated. Let the excess batter drip off, then dredge in breadcrumbs if using. Place the coated florets on the prepared baking sheet in a single layer, ensuring they are not touching.
4. **Bake:** Bake for 20-25 minutes, or until the coating is golden and beginning to crisp.
5. **Prepare the Buffalo Sauce:** While the cauliflower is baking, whisk together the hot sauce, melted vegan butter, and maple syrup in a bowl.
6. **Coat in Sauce:** Remove the cauliflower from the oven and gently toss with the buffalo sauce. Make sure each piece is well coated.
7. **Bake Again:** Return the coated cauliflower to the baking sheet and bake for an additional 20-25 minutes, or until crispy.
8. **Serve:** Let the cauliflower buffalo wings cool slightly before serving. Serve with vegan ranch or blue cheese dressing and celery sticks on the side.

Vegan Quesadillas

 4 servings    50 minutes

INGREDIENTS

- 4 large flour tortillas (use gluten-free if needed)
- 1 cup vegan cheese shreds (choose a brand that melts well)
- 1 can (15 oz) black beans, rinsed and drained
- 1 red bell pepper, thinly sliced
- 1 small red onion, thinly sliced
- 1 cup corn kernels (fresh, canned, or thawed from frozen)
- 1 avocado, sliced
- 1/2 cup fresh cilantro, chopped
- Olive oil or cooking spray for frying
- Salt and pepper, to taste

For Serving:
- Vegan sour cream
- Salsa
- Lime wedges

DIRECTIONS

1. **Prep the Veggies:** Heat a small amount of olive oil in a skillet over medium heat. Add the sliced bell pepper and onion, seasoning with a little salt and pepper. Sauté until they're soft and slightly caramelized, about 5-7 minutes. Add the corn during the last couple of minutes of cooking if you want it to be a bit charred. Set aside.
2. **Assemble the Quesadillas:** Lay out the tortillas on a flat surface. On half of each tortilla, evenly distribute the vegan cheese, followed by the black beans, sautéed bell pepper, onion, corn, and a sprinkle of cilantro. Fold the other half over to close.
3. **Cook the Quesadillas:** Heat a large skillet or griddle over medium heat. Lightly brush with olive oil or spray with cooking spray. Place the filled tortillas in the skillet, cooking in batches if necessary. Cook for 2-3 minutes on each side or until the tortillas are golden brown and crispy, and the cheese has melted.
4. **Serve:** Cut each quesadilla into wedges. Serve hot with avocado slices, vegan sour cream, salsa, and lime wedges on the side.

Edamame with Sea Salt

  4 servings  10 minutes

INGREDIENTS

- 1 pound (450g) frozen edamame in the pod
- 1-2 tablespoons sea salt, or to taste

DIRECTIONS

1. **Cook the Edamame:** Bring a large pot of water to a boil. Add the frozen edamame and cook for 5 to 6 minutes, or until they are tender and bright green. There's no need to thaw the edamame before cooking.
2. **Drain:** Once the edamame is cooked, drain them in a colander and rinse under cold water to stop the cooking process. This also helps to maintain their vibrant green color.
3. **Season:** Transfer the cooked edamame to a large bowl. While they're still warm, sprinkle with sea salt. Toss well to ensure all the pods are lightly coated with salt.
4. **Serve:** Serve the edamame warm or at room temperature. To eat, simply use your teeth to slide the beans out of the pods directly into your mouth. Remember, the pods are not edible.

Vegan Cheese and Crackers

 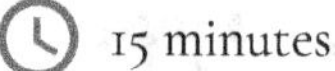

15 minutes

INGREDIENTS

- A selection of vegan cheeses (aim for a variety of textures and flavors, such as soft cashew cheese, aged nut cheese, and flavored vegan spreads)
- An assortment of crackers (choose a mix of flavors and grains, such as whole wheat, seeded, and gluten-free options)
- Fresh fruit (grapes, apple slices, and berries add a fresh, sweet contrast)
- Dried fruit (figs, apricots, and dates offer a chewy texture and natural sweetness)
- Nuts (almonds, walnuts, and cashews provide crunch and richness)
- Olives and pickles (for a briny, tangy element)
- Vegan charcuterie (sliced vegan salami or pepperoni, if desired)

DIRECTIONS

1. **Prepare the Cheese:** Take the vegan cheeses out of the refrigerator about 30 minutes before serving. Many vegan cheeses are best enjoyed at room temperature as their flavors and textures are more pronounced.
2. **Arrange the Platter:** Start by placing the vegan cheeses around a large platter or wooden board. If the cheeses are in large blocks, consider pre-slicing some for easier sampling. Include a separate knife for each cheese to avoid mixing flavors.
3. **Add the Crackers:** Arrange the crackers around the cheeses, grouping similar styles together or mixing them for a varied look. You can also place some crackers in a separate bowl or basket if space is limited.
4. **Incorporate Fruits, Nuts, and Extras:** Fill in the spaces on the platter with fresh and dried fruits, nuts, olives, pickles, and any vegan charcuterie. These components add color, texture, and a range of flavors that complement the vegan cheeses and crackers.
5. **Serve:** Invite your guests to mix and match their bites, creating different combinations of vegan cheese, crackers, and accompaniments. Provide small plates and napkins for convenience.

Vegan Garlic Breadsticks

12 breadsticks  30 minutes

INGREDIENTS

- 1 lb pizza dough (store-bought or homemade, ensure it's vegan)
- 1/4 cup olive oil
- 3 cloves garlic, minced
- 1 teaspoon dried oregano
- 1 teaspoon dried basil
- 1/2 teaspoon sea salt
- 2 tablespoons nutritional yeast (for a cheesy flavor)
- Fresh parsley, chopped (for garnish)

DIRECTIONS

1. **Preheat the Oven:** Preheat your oven to 400°F (200°C). Line a baking sheet with parchment paper.
2. **Prepare the Garlic Oil Mixture:** In a small bowl, combine the olive oil, minced garlic, oregano, basil, and sea salt. Mix well to combine.
3. **Shape the Breadsticks:** On a lightly floured surface, roll out the pizza dough into a rectangle, about 1/2-inch thick. Cut the dough into strips, approximately 1 inch wide.
4. **Apply the Garlic Oil Mixture:** Brush each dough strip generously with the garlic oil mixture. Sprinkle with nutritional yeast for a cheesy taste.
5. **Bake:** Arrange the breadsticks on the prepared baking sheet. Bake in the preheated oven for 12-15 minutes, or until golden brown and crispy.
6. **Garnish and Serve:** Once baked, remove the breadsticks from the oven. Garnish with chopped fresh parsley. Serve warm, with marinara sauce or your favorite vegan dip on the side.

Baked Zucchini Chips

 2-4 servings  2 h 10 minutes

INGREDIENTS

- 2 medium zucchinis
- 1 tablespoon olive oil
- 1/2 teaspoon salt, or to taste
- 1/4 teaspoon ground black pepper, or to taste
- Optional seasonings: garlic powder, smoked paprika, or nutritional yeast for a cheesy flavor

DIRECTIONS

1. **Preheat the Oven:** Preheat your oven to 225°F (105°C). This low temperature helps dehydrate the zucchini slices without burning them. Line a baking sheet with parchment paper.
2. **Prepare the Zucchini:** Wash the zucchinis and slice them into thin rounds, about 1/8 inch thick. A mandoline slicer works best for consistent thickness, but you can also use a sharp knife.
3. **Season the Zucchini:** In a large bowl, toss the zucchini slices with olive oil, salt, pepper, and any other optional seasonings you're using. Ensure each slice is lightly coated.
4. **Arrange the Zucchini Slices:** Place the zucchini slices in a single layer on the prepared baking sheet. Make sure they're not overlapping to ensure even cooking.
5. **Bake:** Bake in the preheated oven for 1.5 to 2 hours, or until the zucchini chips are crispy and golden brown. The baking time may vary depending on the thickness of the slices and the moisture content of the zucchini.
6. **Cool and Serve:** Let the chips cool on the baking sheet to crisp up further. Serve them as a snack or as a side dish.

Crispy Chickpea Snack Mix

 4-6 servings  50 minutes

INGREDIENTS

For the Chickpeas:

- 2 cans (15 oz each) chickpeas, drained, rinsed, and thoroughly dried
- 2 tablespoons olive oil
- 1/2 teaspoon salt
- 1/4 teaspoon ground black pepper

For the Mix:

- 1 cup raw almonds
- 1 cup raw cashews
- 1/2 cup pumpkin seeds
- 1 teaspoon smoked paprika
- 1/2 teaspoon garlic powder
- 1/2 teaspoon onion powder
- 1/4 teaspoon cayenne pepper (adjust to taste)
- Additional salt and pepper, to taste

DIRECTIONS

1. **Roast the Chickpeas:** Preheat your oven to 400°F (200°C). Line a large baking sheet with parchment paper. Toss the chickpeas with olive oil, salt, and pepper until evenly coated. Spread them out in a single layer on the prepared baking sheet. Bake for 20-25 minutes, or until the chickpeas are crispy and golden. Shake the pan or stir halfway through to ensure even roasting.

2. **Add Nuts and Seasonings:** In a large mixing bowl, combine the roasted chickpeas, almonds, cashews, and pumpkin seeds. Sprinkle the smoked paprika, garlic powder, onion powder, cayenne pepper, and additional salt and pepper over the mix. Toss well to ensure everything is evenly coated with the spices.

3. **Final Roast:** Spread the seasoned chickpea and nut mixture back onto the baking sheet in an even layer. Return to the oven and roast for an additional 10-15 minutes, or until the nuts are toasted and fragrant. Be sure to watch closely to prevent burning.

4. **Cool and Serve:** Remove the snack mix from the oven and let it cool completely on the baking sheet. The mixture will crisp up further as it cools.

5. **Storage:** Once cooled, transfer the snack mix to an airtight container. It can be stored at room temperature for up to a week.

Vegan Spinach and Artichoke Dip

 6-8 servings  40 minutes

INGREDIENTS

- 1 cup raw cashews, soaked in hot water for at least 30 minutes then drained
- 1 (14 oz) can artichoke hearts, drained and roughly chopped
- 2 cups fresh spinach, roughly chopped
- 1/2 cup unsweetened almond milk (or any plant-based milk)
- 1/4 cup nutritional yeast for a cheesy flavor
- 2 tablespoons lemon juice
- 2 cloves garlic, minced
- 1/2 teaspoon onion powder
- Salt and pepper, to taste
- Red pepper flakes (optional, for a spicy kick)
- Fresh parsley, chopped (for garnish)

DIRECTIONS

1. **Preheat the Oven:** Preheat your oven to 375°F (190°C).
2. **Blend Cashews:** In a blender or food processor, blend the soaked and drained cashews with almond milk, nutritional yeast, lemon juice, garlic, onion powder, salt, and pepper until smooth and creamy.
3. **Combine Ingredients:** In a mixing bowl, combine the creamy cashew mixture with chopped artichokes and spinach. Mix well. Adjust the seasoning with more salt, pepper, and red pepper flakes if using.
4. **Bake:** Transfer the mixture to a baking dish. Bake in the preheated oven for 20-25 minutes, or until the top is slightly golden and the dip is heated through.
5. **Garnish and Serve:** Garnish with chopped fresh parsley before serving. Serve warm with your choice of toasted bread, crackers, or fresh vegetables for dipping.

Stuffed Mini Portobello Mushrooms

 4 servings    35 minutes

INGREDIENTS

- 12 mini Portobello mushrooms, stems removed and gills scooped out
- 2 tablespoons olive oil, plus more for brushing
- 1 small onion, finely chopped
- 2 cloves garlic, minced
- 1/2 cup breadcrumbs (use gluten-free if necessary)
- 1/4 cup nutritional yeast for a cheesy flavor
- 1/4 cup finely chopped walnuts (optional)
- 1/4 cup fresh parsley, chopped, plus more for garnish
- 1 teaspoon dried thyme
- Salt and pepper, to taste
- 1/4 cup vegetable broth or water, as needed

DIRECTIONS

1. **Preheat the Oven:** Preheat your oven to 375°F (190°C). Line a baking sheet with parchment paper.
2. **Prepare the Mushrooms:** Clean the mushrooms with a damp cloth and remove the stems. Gently scoop out the gills with a spoon. Brush the outside of the mushrooms with olive oil and set them on the prepared baking sheet.
3. **Cook the Filling:** Heat 2 tablespoons of olive oil in a skillet over medium heat. Add the onion and garlic, sautéing until soft and translucent, about 5 minutes. Stir in the breadcrumbs, nutritional yeast, walnuts (if using), parsley, thyme, salt, and pepper. Cook for another 2-3 minutes. If the mixture seems too dry, add a little vegetable broth or water to moisten.
4. **Stuff the Mushrooms:** Spoon the breadcrumb mixture into each mushroom cap, pressing down slightly to compact the filling.
5. **Bake:** Bake in the preheated oven for 15-20 minutes, or until the mushrooms are tender and the tops are golden brown.
6. **Serve:** Garnish with additional chopped parsley before serving. Enjoy warm.

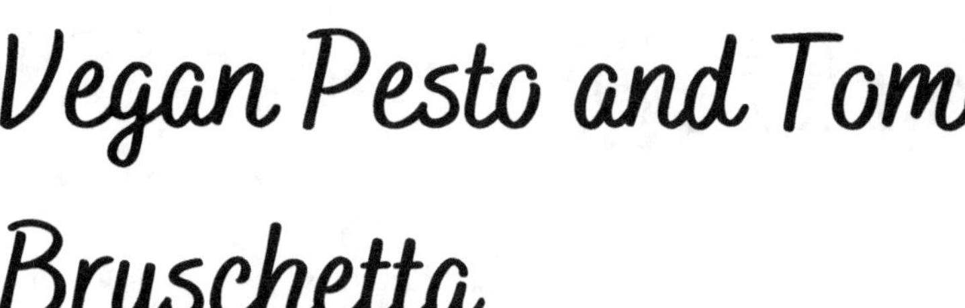# Vegan Pesto and Tomato Bruschetta

🍴 6-8 servings   🕐 23 minutes

INGREDIENTS

- 1 baguette, sliced into 1/2-inch pieces
- 2 tablespoons olive oil, for brushing
- 2 ripe tomatoes, diced
- 1/4 cup red onion, finely chopped
- Salt and pepper, to taste
- Fresh basil leaves, for garnish

For the Vegan Pesto:
- 2 cups fresh basil leaves
- 1/2 cup pine nuts (or walnuts)
- 3 cloves garlic
- 1/2 cup olive oil
- 1/4 cup nutritional yeast
- Salt and pepper, to taste
- Juice of 1/2 lemon

DIRECTIONS

1. **Make the Vegan Pesto:** In a food processor, combine the basil leaves, pine nuts, garlic, nutritional yeast, and lemon juice. Pulse until coarsely chopped. With the processor running, gradually add the olive oil until the pesto reaches your desired consistency. Season with salt and pepper to taste. Set aside.
2. **Prepare the Bruschetta Topping:** In a bowl, mix together the diced tomatoes and red onion. Season with salt and pepper. Let it sit for a few minutes to meld the flavors.
3. **Toast the Bread:** Preheat your oven to 400°F (200°C). Arrange the baguette slices on a baking sheet and lightly brush each piece with olive oil. Toast in the oven for 5-8 minutes, or until the edges are golden and crispy. Remove and let cool slightly.
4. **Assemble the Bruschetta:** Spread a generous amount of vegan pesto on each toasted baguette slice. Top with the tomato and onion mixture.
5. **Serve:** Garnish each bruschetta with a fresh basil leaf. Serve immediately.

Roasted Red Beet Hummus

 4-6 servings  70 minutes

INGREDIENTS

- 1 medium red beet, scrubbed and trimmed
- 1 can (15 oz) chickpeas, drained and rinsed
- 3 tablespoons tahini
- 2 cloves garlic
- Juice of 1 lemon
- 2 tablespoons olive oil, plus more for roasting and serving
- Salt and pepper, to taste
- 1/2 teaspoon ground cumin (optional)
- Water, as needed for blending
- Fresh parsley, chopped, for garnish
- Toasted sesame seeds, for garnish

DIRECTIONS

1. **Roast the Beet:** Preheat your oven to 400°F (200°C). Wrap the beet in foil with a drizzle of olive oil and a pinch of salt. Place on a baking sheet and roast in the oven for 50-60 minutes, or until tender and easily pierced with a fork. Once cooled, peel the beet and chop it into chunks.
2. **Blend the Hummus:** In a food processor, combine the roasted beet chunks, chickpeas, tahini, garlic, lemon juice, olive oil, salt, pepper, and cumin (if using). Blend until smooth. If the hummus is too thick, add water, one tablespoon at a time, until you reach your desired consistency.
3. **Serve:** Transfer the hummus to a serving bowl. Create a swirl on the top using the back of a spoon. Drizzle with a little olive oil, and sprinkle with chopped parsley and toasted sesame seeds for garnish.
4. **Enjoy:** Serve with pita bread, crackers, or a selection of fresh vegetables for dipping.

Sweet Potato and Avocado Bites

 4-6 servings  40 minutes

INGREDIENTS

- 2 large sweet potatoes, peeled and cut into 1/2-inch thick rounds
- 2 tablespoons olive oil
- Salt and pepper, to taste
- 2 ripe avocados, peeled and mashed
- Juice of 1 lime, divided
- 1 small red onion, finely chopped
- 1/4 cup fresh cilantro, chopped, plus extra for garnish
- 1/4 teaspoon chili powder (optional for a bit of heat)
- Paprika or smoked paprika, for garnish

DIRECTIONS

1. **Roast the Sweet Potatoes:** Preheat your oven to 400°F (200°C). Line a baking sheet with parchment paper. Toss the sweet potato rounds with olive oil, salt, and pepper. Arrange them in a single layer on the prepared baking sheet. Roast for 20-25 minutes, flipping halfway through, until they are tender and slightly golden at the edges. Let them cool slightly.
2. **Prepare the Avocado Mixture:** In a medium bowl, combine the mashed avocados, half of the lime juice, chopped red onion, cilantro, and chili powder (if using). Season with salt and pepper to taste. Mix well until smooth.
3. **Assemble the Bites:** Place the roasted sweet potato rounds on a serving platter. Top each round with a spoonful of the avocado mixture.
4. **Garnish and Serve:** Drizzle the remaining lime juice over the assembled bites. Sprinkle with paprika and garnish with additional cilantro leaves. Serve immediately or chill in the refrigerator for 30 minutes before serving for a refreshing appetizer.

Vegan Buffalo Cauliflower Tots

 4-6 servings    45 minutes

INGREDIENTS

- 1 medium head of cauliflower, cut into florets
- 1/2 cup water
- 1/2 cup unsweetened almond milk (or any plant-based milk)
- 3/4 cup all-purpose flour (for gluten-free, use a gluten-free flour blend)
- 1 teaspoon garlic powder
- 1/2 teaspoon onion powder
- Salt and pepper, to taste
- 1 cup panko breadcrumbs (use gluten-free if needed)
- 1/2 cup vegan buffalo sauce
- 2 tablespoons vegan butter, melted
- Ranch dressing (vegan), for serving
- Celery sticks, for serving

DIRECTIONS

1. **Preheat the Oven and Prepare Baking Sheet:** Preheat your oven to 450°F (230°C). Line a baking sheet with parchment paper or a silicone mat.
2. **Blanch the Cauliflower:** Bring a large pot of water to a boil. Blanch the cauliflower florets for about 2 minutes. Drain and let them cool slightly.
3. **Prepare the Batter:** In a large bowl, whisk together the water, almond milk, flour, garlic powder, onion powder, salt, and pepper until smooth. The batter should be thick enough to coat the florets but not too runny.
4. **Bread the Cauliflower:** Dip each cauliflower floret into the batter, shaking off the excess. Roll the battered florets in panko breadcrumbs until well coated, then place them on the prepared baking sheet. Repeat with all the florets.
5. **Bake:** Bake for 20-25 minutes, or until the tots are golden and crispy, flipping halfway through the baking time.
6. **Toss with Buffalo Sauce:** While the tots are baking, mix the vegan buffalo sauce with melted vegan butter in a large bowl. Once the tots are baked, toss them in the buffalo sauce mixture until evenly coated. Return the coated tots to the baking sheet.
7. **Broil (Optional):** For extra crispiness, broil the coated tots for 2-3 minutes, watching closely to prevent burning.
8. **Serve:** Serve the Vegan Buffalo Cauliflower Tots hot with vegan ranch dressing and celery sticks on the side.

Lunch

Vegan BLT Sandwich

 2 servings    20 minutes

INGREDIENTS

For the Vegan Bacon:

- 8 slices of your preferred vegan bacon (tempeh bacon, tofu bacon, or mushroom bacon)
- Olive oil or cooking spray (if required based on your vegan bacon choice)

For the Sandwich:

- 4 slices of bread (whole grain, sourdough, or your favorite type), toasted
- 1/4 cup vegan mayonnaise
- 4 lettuce leaves (romaine, iceberg, or butter lettuce work well)
- 1 large tomato, sliced
- Salt and pepper, to taste
- Optional: Avocado slices or sprouts for added freshness and texture

DIRECTIONS

1. **Cook the Vegan Bacon:** Prepare the vegan bacon according to its recipe or the instructions on the package. Typically, this involves pan-frying until crispy, but methods may vary. Set aside on paper towels to drain any excess oil.
2. **Toast the Bread:** Lightly toast the bread slices until golden and crispy. This adds texture and prevents the bread from becoming soggy from the tomato or vegan mayo.
3. **Assemble the Sandwich:** Spread a generous amount of vegan mayonnaise on one side of each slice of toasted bread. On two slices of bread, layer the lettuce leaves, followed by the tomato slices. Season the tomato slices with a pinch of salt and pepper.
4. **Add Vegan Bacon and Optional Extras:** Place the cooked vegan bacon on top of the tomatoes. If using, add avocado slices or sprouts for an extra layer of flavor and texture.
5. **Complete the Sandwich:** Top with the remaining slices of bread, mayo-side down. Press gently to secure the ingredients.
6. **Serve:** Cut the sandwiches in half, if desired, and serve immediately for the best taste and texture.

Chickpea Salad Sandwich

☆☆☆☆☆

 2 servings    15 minutes

INGREDIENTS

For the Chickpea Salad:

- 1 can (15 oz) chickpeas, drained and rinsed
- 1/4 cup vegan mayonnaise
- 1 tablespoon Dijon mustard
- 1 tablespoon lemon juice
- 1/4 cup red onion, finely chopped
- 1/4 cup celery, finely chopped
- 1/4 cup pickles or pickle relish, chopped (optional)
- Salt and pepper, to taste
- 1/4 teaspoon paprika (optional for a smoky flavor)
- 1 tablespoon fresh dill or parsley, chopped (optional)

For the Sandwich:

- 4 slices of your favorite bread, toasted if preferred
- Lettuce leaves
- Tomato slices
- Additional vegan mayonnaise (for spreading on the bread)
- Avocado slices (optional)

DIRECTIONS

1. **Mash the Chickpeas:** In a medium bowl, use a fork or potato masher to roughly mash the chickpeas. They should be broken down but still have some texture.
2. **Make the Salad:** To the mashed chickpeas, add the vegan mayonnaise, Dijon mustard, lemon juice, red onion, celery, pickles (if using), salt, pepper, and paprika (if using). Mix well to combine. Stir in the fresh dill or parsley, if using.
3. **Assemble the Sandwich:** Spread additional vegan mayonnaise on one side of each bread slice, if desired. On two slices of bread, layer lettuce leaves and tomato slices. Divide the chickpea salad between the sandwiches, spreading it evenly over the tomatoes. Add avocado slices if using.
4. **Complete and Serve:** Top with the remaining slices of bread. Press down gently, then cut the sandwiches in half.
5. **Enjoy!** Serve the chickpea salad sandwiches immediately, or wrap them up for an on-the-go meal.

Vegan Sushi Rolls

 4-6 servings    1 hour

INGREDIENTS

For the Sushi Rice:

- 2 cups sushi rice
- 2 1/2 cups water
- 1/4 cup rice vinegar
- 2 tablespoons sugar
- 1/2 teaspoon salt

For the Filling:

- Avocado, sliced
- Cucumber, julienned
- Carrot, julienned and blanched if desired
- Bell pepper, julienned
- Asparagus, blanched
- Spinach, blanched
- Tofu, pan-fried and cut into strips
- Pickled radish (optional)

Additional:

- Nori (seaweed) sheets
- Soy sauce, for dipping
- Wasabi and pickled ginger, for serving
- A bamboo sushi mat for rolling

DIRECTIONS

1. **Prepare the Sushi Rice:** Rinse the sushi rice under cold water until the water runs clear. Combine the rice and 2 1/2 cups of water in a rice cooker and cook according to the manufacturer's instructions. Alternatively, cook the rice in a pot with a tight-fitting lid: bring to a boil, then reduce heat to low, cover, and cook for 20 minutes. Remove from heat and let it sit, covered, for 10 minutes. Heat the rice vinegar, sugar, and salt in a small saucepan until the sugar dissolves. Cool to room temperature. Transfer the cooked rice to a large bowl and gently fold in the vinegar mixture. Allow the rice to cool to room temperature, uncovered.

2. **Prepare the Fillings:** Prepare your chosen fillings by slicing them into long, thin strips. Blanching vegetables like carrots and asparagus can make them more pliable and easier to roll.

3. **Assemble the Sushi Rolls:** Place a nori sheet shiny-side down on your bamboo mat. With wet hands, spread a thin layer of sushi rice over the nori, leaving about a 1/2-inch border at the top. Arrange your chosen fillings in a line at the bottom of the rice-covered nori. Lift the edge of the bamboo mat closest to you and roll it away from you, pressing gently but firmly. Use the mat to shape the roll. Continue rolling until the edges seal together with the help of the rice's stickiness. With a sharp knife, cut the roll into bite-sized pieces. Wet the knife between cuts to prevent sticking.

4. **Serve:** Arrange the sushi rolls on a platter. Serve with soy sauce for dipping, and wasabi and pickled ginger on the side.

Quinoa and Black Bean Tacos

 4-6 servings  30 minutes

INGREDIENTS

For the Quinoa and Black Bean Mixture:

- 1 cup quinoa, rinsed
- 2 cups vegetable broth or water
- 1 can (15 oz) black beans, drained and rinsed
- 1 tablespoon olive oil
- 1 small onion, finely diced
- 2 cloves garlic, minced
- 1 teaspoon ground cumin
- 1/2 teaspoon chili powder
- 1/4 teaspoon smoked paprika (optional)
- Salt and pepper, to taste
- Juice of 1 lime

For Serving:

- Corn or flour tortillas, warmed
- Diced avocado or guacamole
- Chopped fresh cilantro
- Sliced radishes
- Diced tomatoes
- Shredded lettuce or cabbage
- Vegan sour cream or yogurt
- Lime wedges
- Hot sauce or salsa

DIRECTIONS

1. **Cook the Quinoa:** In a medium saucepan, bring the vegetable broth (or water) to a boil. Add the rinsed quinoa, reduce heat to low, cover, and simmer for about 15 minutes, or until the liquid is absorbed and the quinoa is tender. Remove from heat and let it sit, covered, for 5 minutes. Fluff with a fork.

2. **Sauté the Onion and Garlic:** While the quinoa is cooking, heat the olive oil in a large skillet over medium heat. Add the diced onion and cook until soft and translucent, about 5 minutes. Add the minced garlic and cook for another minute until fragrant.

3. **Combine Quinoa and Black Beans:** Add the cooked quinoa and rinsed black beans to the skillet with the onion and garlic. Stir in the ground cumin, chili powder, smoked paprika, salt, and pepper. Cook for a few minutes until the mixture is heated through. Remove from heat and stir in the lime juice.

4. **Assemble the Tacos:** Spoon the quinoa and black bean mixture into the warmed tortillas. Top with diced avocado, chopped cilantro, sliced radishes, diced tomatoes, shredded lettuce, vegan sour cream, and any other toppings of your choice.

5. **Serve:** Serve the tacos immediately, with lime wedges and hot sauce or salsa on the side.

Vegan Buddha Bowl

🍴 2-4 servings 🕐 45 minutes

INGREDIENTS

For the Bowl:

- 1 cup quinoa or brown rice, cooked according to package instructions
- 1 can (15 oz) chickpeas, drained, rinsed, and roasted
- 1 avocado, sliced
- 1 cup purple cabbage, shredded
- 1 carrot, julienned or grated
- 1 small beet, julienned or grated
- 1/2 cup cucumbers, sliced
- 1/2 cup sweet corn (canned, fresh, or frozen and thawed)
- 1 cup spinach or mixed greens
- 1/4 cup pumpkin seeds or sunflower seeds
- Optional: sprouts, microgreens, or sliced radishes for extra crunch

For the Roasted Chickpeas:

- 1 tablespoon olive oil
- 1/2 teaspoon smoked paprika
- 1/2 teaspoon ground cumin
- Salt and pepper, to taste

For the Dressing:

- 1/4 cup tahini
- 2 tablespoons lemon juice
- 1 tablespoon maple syrup or agave nectar
- 1 clove garlic, minced
- Water, as needed to achieve desired consistency
- Salt and pepper, to taste

DIRECTIONS

1. **Prepare the Roasted Chickpeas:** Preheat the oven to 400°F (200°C). Toss the chickpeas with olive oil, smoked paprika, ground cumin, salt, and pepper. Spread on a baking sheet and roast for 20-25 minutes, or until crispy. Shake the pan halfway through for even cooking.

2. **Assemble the Bowls:** Divide the cooked quinoa or brown rice among bowls as the base. Arrange the sliced avocado, shredded cabbage, julienned carrot and beet, sliced cucumbers, sweet corn, spinach or mixed greens, and roasted chickpeas on top. Sprinkle with pumpkin seeds or sunflower seeds, and add any optional ingredients like sprouts or radishes.

3. **Make the Dressing:** Whisk together tahini, lemon juice, maple syrup, minced garlic, salt, and pepper in a small bowl. Add water, a tablespoon at a time, until the dressing reaches a pourable consistency.

4. **Serve:** Drizzle the dressing over each bowl just before serving. Toss everything together to mix the flavors and enjoy!

Grilled Vegetable Wrap

 4 servings    30 minutes

INGREDIENTS

For the Grilled Vegetables:

- 1 zucchini, sliced lengthwise
- 1 yellow squash, sliced lengthwise
- 1 red bell pepper, seeded and quartered
- 1 yellow bell pepper, seeded and quartered
- 1 red onion, sliced into rings
- 2 tablespoons olive oil
- Salt and pepper, to taste

For the Wrap:

- 4 large tortillas (whole wheat, spinach, or gluten-free, as preferred)
- 1/2 cup hummus or vegan pesto
- 1 cup baby spinach or mixed greens
- 1 avocado, sliced
- Optional: fresh herbs like basil or cilantro, sprouts, or a sprinkle of nutritional yeast

DIRECTIONS

1. **Grill the Vegetables:** Preheat your grill or grill pan to medium-high heat. Toss the sliced zucchini, yellow squash, bell peppers, and red onion with olive oil, salt, and pepper in a large bowl until evenly coated. Grill the vegetables for about 4-6 minutes per side, or until tender and charred to your liking. Remove from the grill and let them cool slightly.

2. **Prepare the Wraps:** Lay out the tortillas on a clean surface. Spread each tortilla evenly with hummus or vegan pesto. On one side of each tortilla, arrange a layer of baby spinach or mixed greens. Top with the grilled vegetables and avocado slices. If using, add fresh herbs, sprouts, or a sprinkle of nutritional yeast.

3. **Wrap It Up:** Carefully roll up the tortillas, tucking in the sides as you go, to enclose the filling. If desired, you can lightly grill the wraps on the grill pan for 1-2 minutes on each side to warm the tortilla and create grill marks.

4. **Serve:** Cut the wraps in half diagonally and serve immediately.

Vegan Pasta Salad

 6-8 servings    30 minutes

INGREDIENTS

For the Pasta Salad:

- 8 oz (about 225g) pasta (choose shapes like penne, fusilli, or farfalle, and opt for whole wheat or gluten-free if desired)
- 1 cup cherry tomatoes, halved
- 1 cucumber, diced
- 1 bell pepper (any color), diced
- 1/2 red onion, thinly sliced
- 1 can (15 oz) chickpeas, drained and rinsed
- 1/2 cup olives, sliced (Kalamata or black olives)
- 1/4 cup sun-dried tomatoes, chopped (optional)
- 1/2 cup artichoke hearts, chopped (optional)
- 1/4 cup fresh basil leaves, chopped
- Salt and pepper, to taste

For the Dressing:

- 1/3 cup olive oil
- 3 tablespoons red wine vinegar or apple cider vinegar
- 2 tablespoons lemon juice
- 1 teaspoon Dijon mustard
- 1 clove garlic, minced
- 1 teaspoon dried oregano
- Salt and pepper, to taste

DIRECTIONS

1. **Cook the Pasta:** Bring a large pot of salted water to a boil. Add the pasta and cook according to the package instructions until al dente. Drain and rinse under cold water to cool. Transfer to a large mixing bowl.
2. **Prepare the Vegetables and Add-ins:** Add the cherry tomatoes, cucumber, bell pepper, red onion, chickpeas, olives, sun-dried tomatoes, artichoke hearts, and chopped basil to the bowl with the cooled pasta. Toss to combine.
3. **Make the Dressing:** In a small bowl, whisk together the olive oil, vinegar, lemon juice, Dijon mustard, minced garlic, oregano, salt, and pepper until well combined.
4. **Combine and Chill:** Pour the dressing over the pasta salad and toss until everything is evenly coated. Season with additional salt and pepper to taste. For the best flavor, cover and chill in the refrigerator for at least 1 hour before serving.
5. **Serve:** Give the pasta salad a good stir before serving. Garnish with additional fresh basil if desired. Enjoy chilled or at room temperature.

BBQ Jackfruit Sandwiches

☆☆☆☆☆

 4-6 servings    45 minutes

INGREDIENTS

For the BBQ Jackfruit:

- 2 cans (20 oz each) young green jackfruit in water or brine, drained and rinsed
- 1 tablespoon olive oil
- 1 small onion, finely chopped
- 2 cloves garlic, minced
- 1 teaspoon smoked paprika
- 1/2 teaspoon chili powder
- 1/2 teaspoon ground cumin
- Salt and pepper, to taste
- 1 cup BBQ sauce (vegan-friendly)
- 1/2 cup vegetable broth

For the Coleslaw:

- 2 cups shredded cabbage (green, red, or a mix)
- 1 carrot, shredded
- 1/4 cup vegan mayonnaise
- 1 tablespoon apple cider vinegar
- 1 teaspoon Dijon mustard
- 1 teaspoon maple syrup or sugar
- Salt and pepper, to taste

Additional:

- 4-6 burger buns, toasted (ensure vegan-friendly)
- Pickles or additional toppings, as desired

DIRECTIONS

1. **Prepare the Jackfruit:** Use your fingers or a fork to shred the jackfruit pieces to mimic the texture of pulled pork. In a large skillet, heat the olive oil over medium heat. Add the chopped onion and cook until softened, about 5 minutes. Add the minced garlic, smoked paprika, chili powder, ground cumin, salt, and pepper, and cook for another 1-2 minutes, until fragrant. Add the shredded jackfruit, BBQ sauce, and vegetable broth to the skillet. Stir well to combine. Reduce the heat to low, cover, and simmer for 20-25 minutes, stirring occasionally, until the jackfruit is tender and has absorbed the flavors. If the mixture becomes too dry, add a little more broth or BBQ sauce.

2. **Make the Coleslaw:** In a large bowl, combine the shredded cabbage, shredded carrot, vegan mayonnaise, apple cider vinegar, Dijon mustard, maple syrup, salt, and pepper. Mix until the vegetables are well coated in the dressing. Adjust seasoning to taste. Set aside to marinate while the jackfruit cooks.

3. **Assemble the Sandwiches:** Spoon a generous amount of the BBQ jackfruit onto the bottom halves of the toasted burger buns. Top with a heaping spoonful of coleslaw. Add any additional toppings like pickles if desired, then cover with the top halves of the buns.

4. **Serve:** Serve the BBQ Jackfruit Sandwiches immediately, accompanied by extra BBQ sauce or pickles on the side.

Vegan Caesar Wrap

 4 servings    20 minutes

INGREDIENTS

For the Vegan Caesar Dressing:

- 1/2 cup raw cashews, soaked for 4 hours or overnight and drained
- 1/4 cup water (more if needed for blending)
- 2 tablespoons lemon juice
- 1 tablespoon nutritional yeast
- 1 tablespoon Dijon mustard
- 1 clove garlic
- 1 teaspoon capers
- Salt and pepper, to taste

For the Wrap:

- 4 large tortillas (whole wheat, spinach, or gluten-free)
- 4 cups romaine lettuce, chopped
- 1 cup cherry tomatoes, halved
- 1/2 cucumber, thinly sliced
- 1 avocado, sliced
- 1/4 red onion, thinly sliced
- Optional: Crumbled tofu or chickpeas for added protein
- Optional: Vegan parmesan cheese for garnish

DIRECTIONS

1. **Make the Vegan Caesar Dressing:** In a blender, combine the soaked and drained cashews, water, lemon juice, nutritional yeast, Dijon mustard, garlic, capers, salt, and pepper. Blend until smooth and creamy. Adjust the seasoning to taste and add more water if necessary to reach your desired consistency.

2. **Assemble the Wraps:** Lay out the tortillas on a clean surface. Spread a generous amount of the vegan Caesar dressing over each tortilla. In the center of each tortilla, layer the chopped romaine lettuce, cherry tomatoes, cucumber slices, avocado slices, and red onion. If using, add crumbled tofu, chickpeas, or a sprinkle of vegan parmesan cheese. Drizzle with additional Caesar dressing if desired.

3. **Wrap and Serve:** Carefully fold in the sides of each tortilla, then roll tightly to enclose the filling. If necessary, you can secure the wraps with toothpicks. Serve immediately, or wrap in foil for an on-the-go meal.

Falafel and Hummus Pita

 4 servings  1 hour

INGREDIENTS

For the Falafel:

- 1 cup dried chickpeas, soaked overnight (do not use canned chickpeas as they're too soft)
- 1 small onion, roughly chopped
- 2-3 garlic cloves, minced
- 1/4 cup fresh parsley, chopped
- 1/4 cup fresh cilantro, chopped
- 1 teaspoon ground cumin
- 1 teaspoon ground coriander
- 1/2 teaspoon cayenne pepper (adjust to taste)
- 1/2 teaspoon baking soda
- Salt and pepper, to taste
- Vegetable oil, for frying

Additional Ingredients:

- 4 pita breads, warmed
- 1 cup hummus
- 1 tomato, diced
- 1 cucumber, sliced
- 1/4 red onion, thinly sliced
- Lettuce leaves
- Optional: tzatziki or tahini sauce, pickles, olives

DIRECTIONS

1. **Make the Falafel:** Drain and rinse the soaked chickpeas. In a food processor, combine the chickpeas, onion, garlic, parsley, cilantro, cumin, coriander, cayenne, baking soda, salt, and pepper. Pulse until the mixture is finely ground but not pureed. Shape the mixture into small balls or patties, about the size of a walnut. Heat about an inch of vegetable oil in a deep skillet over medium heat. Fry the falafel in batches, turning them occasionally, until golden brown and crispy, about 4-5 minutes. Drain on paper towels.

2. **Assemble the Pitas:** Cut each pita bread in half to form pockets. Spread a generous amount of hummus inside each pita half. Stuff with falafel balls (2-3 per pita half), diced tomato, cucumber slices, red onion, and lettuce leaves. If using, drizzle with tzatziki or tahini sauce and add pickles or olives as desired.

3. **Serve:** Serve the falafel and hummus pitas immediately, with extra hummus, tzatziki, or tahini sauce on the side for dipping.

Vegan Tempeh Reuben Sandwich

☆☆☆☆☆

 2 sandwiches  50 minutes

INGREDIENTS

For the Tempeh Marinade:
- 8 oz tempeh, sliced thinly
- 1/2 cup vegetable broth
- 2 tablespoons soy sauce or tamari
- 1 tablespoon apple cider vinegar
- 1 teaspoon smoked paprika
- 1 teaspoon garlic powder
- 1/2 teaspoon ground black pepper

For the Vegan Russian Dressing:
- 1/2 cup vegan mayonnaise
- 2 tablespoons ketchup
- 1 tablespoon finely chopped pickles or pickle relish
- 1 teaspoon hot sauce (adjust to taste)
- Salt and pepper, to taste

For the Sandwich:
- Rye bread, 4 slices
- 1 cup sauerkraut, drained
- Vegan cheese slices (optional)
- 1 tablespoon olive oil or vegan butter, for grilling

DIRECTIONS

1. **Marinate the Tempeh:** In a shallow dish, whisk together the vegetable broth, soy sauce, apple cider vinegar, smoked paprika, garlic powder, and black pepper. Add the tempeh slices, ensuring they are fully submerged. Marinate for at least 30 minutes, or for better flavor, overnight in the refrigerator.
2. **Prepare the Vegan Russian Dressing:** In a small bowl, mix together the vegan mayonnaise, ketchup, chopped pickles, hot sauce, salt, and pepper until smooth. Set aside.
3. **Cook the Tempeh:** Heat olive oil or vegan butter in a skillet over medium heat. Remove tempeh from the marinade and cook until browned on both sides, about 3-4 minutes per side.
4. **Assemble the Sandwich:** Spread a generous amount of the vegan Russian dressing on one side of each slice of rye bread. On two slices of bread, layer the cooked tempeh, sauerkraut, and vegan cheese slices (if using). Top with the remaining slices of bread, dressing side down.
5. **Grill the Sandwich:** Heat a panini press or a skillet over medium heat. If using a skillet, press down with a spatula or another heavy pan to flatten the sandwiches slightly. Grill until the bread is toasted and crispy, and the cheese (if using) is melted, about 5 minutes.
6. **Serve:** Cut the sandwiches in half and serve hot.

Spicy Vegan Peanut Noodles

4 servings · 25 minutes

INGREDIENTS

- 8 oz noodles (rice noodles, soba, or spaghetti work well)
- 1 red bell pepper, thinly sliced
- 1 carrot, julienned or grated
- 1 cucumber, julienned (optional)
- 2 green onions, thinly sliced
- 1/4 cup cilantro, chopped (optional for garnish)
- 1/4 cup crushed peanuts, for garnish

For the Spicy Peanut Sauce:
- 1/2 cup natural peanut butter (smooth or crunchy)
- 1/4 cup soy sauce or tamari (for gluten-free option)
- 2 tablespoons maple syrup or agave nectar
- 2 tablespoons rice vinegar
- 1 tablespoon sesame oil
- 1-2 teaspoons chili sauce (such as Sriracha), adjust to taste
- 2 cloves garlic, minced
- 1 inch piece ginger, grated
- Water, as needed to thin the sauce

DIRECTIONS

1. **Cook the Noodles:** Prepare the noodles according to package instructions. Drain and rinse under cold water if serving cold. Set aside.
2. **Prepare the Vegetables:** Prepare the red bell pepper, carrot, cucumber, and green onions as directed. Set aside.
3. **Make the Spicy Peanut Sauce:** In a bowl, whisk together peanut butter, soy sauce, maple syrup, rice vinegar, sesame oil, chili sauce, minced garlic, and grated ginger until smooth. If the sauce is too thick, whisk in a little water until you achieve the desired consistency.
4. **Combine Noodles and Vegetables:** In a large mixing bowl, toss the cooked noodles with the prepared vegetables.
5. **Dress the Noodles:** Pour the spicy peanut sauce over the noodle and vegetable mixture. Toss well to ensure everything is evenly coated with the sauce.
6. **Serve:** Serve the noodles garnished with sliced green onions, chopped cilantro, and crushed peanuts. Enjoy warm or chill in the refrigerator before serving cold.

Vegan Mediterranean Wrap

☆☆☆☆☆

 2-4 servings    15 minutes

INGREDIENTS

- Large whole wheat or spinach tortillas
- 1/2 cup hummus (homemade or store-bought)
- 1 cup mixed salad greens or baby spinach
- 1 small cucumber, thinly sliced
- 1/2 red bell pepper, thinly sliced
- 1/4 red onion, thinly sliced
- 1/4 cup Kalamata olives, pitted and sliced
- 1/4 cup sun-dried tomatoes in oil, drained and chopped
- 1/4 cup artichoke hearts in water, drained and chopped
- 1/4 cup crumbled vegan feta cheese (optional)
- Salt and pepper, to taste
- A drizzle of olive oil and balsamic vinegar (optional)

DIRECTIONS

1. **Prepare the Ingredients:** Wash and slice the cucumber, red bell pepper, and red onion. Drain and chop the sun-dried tomatoes and artichoke hearts. Set everything aside.
2. **Assemble the Wrap:** Lay out a tortilla on a flat surface. Spread a generous layer of hummus over the entire surface of the tortilla. On one side of the tortilla, arrange a handful of salad greens or baby spinach. Top with slices of cucumber, red bell pepper, red onion, Kalamata olives, sun-dried tomatoes, artichoke hearts, and vegan feta cheese, if using. If desired, drizzle a little olive oil and balsamic vinegar over the filling for added flavor. Season with salt and pepper to taste.
3. **Wrap It Up:** Carefully fold the sides of the tortilla inwards, then roll it up tightly from the bottom to encase the fillings. If necessary, use a toothpick to secure the wrap.
4. **Serve:** The wrap can be enjoyed immediately or wrapped in foil/parchment paper for a grab-and-go meal. For a crispy exterior, you can also grill the wrap on a panini press or in a skillet for a few minutes on each side until golden.

Quinoa Stuffed Avocados

4 stuffed avocado halves   15 minutes

INGREDIENTS

- 2 ripe avocados, halved and pits removed
- 1 cup cooked quinoa (cool to room temperature)
- 1/2 cup cherry tomatoes, halved or quartered
- 1/4 cup black beans, rinsed and drained
- 1/4 cup corn kernels (fresh, canned, or thawed if frozen)
- 2 tablespoons red onion, finely chopped
- 2 tablespoons cilantro, chopped (plus more for garnish)
- Juice of 1 lime
- Salt and pepper, to taste
- Optional: Chili flakes or sliced jalapeño for heat, crumbled vegan feta for creaminess

Dressing (Optional):

- 3 tablespoons olive oil
- 1 tablespoon lime juice
- 1 teaspoon maple syrup or agave nectar
- Salt and pepper, to taste
- A pinch of garlic powder

DIRECTIONS

1. **Prepare the Filling:** In a medium bowl, combine the cooked quinoa, cherry tomatoes, black beans, corn kernels, red onion, and chopped cilantro. Drizzle with the juice of 1 lime, then season with salt and pepper to taste. Mix well to combine. Adjust seasoning and lime juice as necessary.
2. **Make the Dressing (Optional):** In a small bowl, whisk together olive oil, lime juice, maple syrup, salt, pepper, and garlic powder until well combined.
3. **Stuff the Avocados:** Scoop out a little flesh from the center of each avocado half to create more space for the filling, if necessary. (The scooped-out avocado can be mashed and mixed into the quinoa filling.) Spoon the quinoa mixture into the avocado halves, packing it lightly.
4. **Add Dressing and Garnish:** Drizzle the optional dressing over the stuffed avocados. Garnish with additional cilantro, chili flakes, sliced jalapeño, or crumbled vegan feta, if using.
5. **Serve:** Serve immediately, with extra lime wedges on the side if desired.

Vegan "Egg" Salad Sandwich

2-4 sandwiches 15 minutes

INGREDIENTS

- 1 block (14 oz) firm tofu, pressed and crumbled
- 1/4 cup vegan mayonnaise
- 1 tablespoon Dijon mustard
- 1/4 teaspoon turmeric (for color)
- 1/2 teaspoon black salt (kala namak) (for an eggy flavor)
- 1/2 teaspoon onion powder
- 1/2 teaspoon garlic powder
- Freshly ground black pepper, to taste
- 1/4 cup celery, finely chopped
- 1/4 cup red onion, finely chopped
- 2 tablespoons fresh chives, chopped (optional)
- Bread slices (your choice)
- Lettuce leaves and sliced tomatoes (for serving)

DIRECTIONS

1. **Crumble the Tofu:** Drain and press the tofu to remove excess water. Crumble the tofu into a mixing bowl, mimicking the texture of chopped hard-boiled eggs.
2. **Mix the "Egg" Salad:** To the crumbled tofu, add vegan mayonnaise, Dijon mustard, turmeric, black salt, onion powder, garlic powder, and black pepper. Mix well until the tofu is evenly coated. Gently fold in the chopped celery, red onion, and chives (if using) until well combined. Adjust seasoning to taste.
3. **Assemble the Sandwich:** Toast the bread slices if desired. Spoon a generous amount of the tofu "egg" salad onto one slice of bread. Add lettuce and tomato slices on top, then cover with another slice of bread.
4. **Serve:** Cut the sandwich in half and serve immediately, or wrap it up for a grab-and-go lunch.

Mushroom and Black Bean Burgers

🍴 4-6 burgers   🕐 30 minutes

INGREDIENTS

- 1 can (15 oz) black beans, drained and rinsed
- 2 cups mushrooms (such as cremini or button), finely chopped
- 1/2 cup rolled oats, ground into a flour
- 1/4 cup breadcrumbs (use gluten-free if needed)
- 1 small onion, finely chopped
- 2 cloves garlic, minced
- 1 tablespoon soy sauce or tamari (for a gluten-free option)
- 1 teaspoon smoked paprika
- 1 teaspoon cumin
- Salt and pepper, to taste
- 2 tablespoons olive oil, for cooking
- Burger buns (ensure they're vegan)
- Toppings: lettuce, tomato, vegan mayonnaise, mustard, ketchup, avocado slices, etc.

DIRECTIONS

1. **Mash the Black Beans:** In a large bowl, use a fork or potato masher to partially mash the black beans. Leave some beans whole for texture.
2. **Cook the Mushrooms:** Heat 1 tablespoon of olive oil in a skillet over medium heat. Add the chopped mushrooms, onion, and garlic. Cook until the mushrooms have released their moisture and the onions are soft, about 5-7 minutes. Let cool slightly.
3. **Prepare the Burger Mixture:** To the bowl with the mashed black beans, add the cooked mushroom mixture, ground oats, breadcrumbs, soy sauce, smoked paprika, cumin, salt, and pepper. Mix well until combined. If the mixture feels too wet, add a little more oat flour or breadcrumbs.
4. **Form the Patties:** Divide the mixture into 4-6 equal portions, depending on your preferred patty size. Shape into patties.
5. **Cook the Burgers:** Heat the remaining olive oil in a skillet over medium heat. Cook the patties for 4-5 minutes on each side, or until they are golden brown and heated through. Alternatively, grill the patties on a preheated grill over medium heat, ensuring they don't stick.
6. **Assemble the Burgers:** Toast the burger buns, then spread your choice of vegan mayonnaise, mustard, or ketchup on the bottom bun. Place a cooked patty on each bun and top with lettuce, tomato, avocado slices, or any other desired toppings. Cap with the top bun.
7. **Serve:** Serve the Mushroom and Black Bean Burgers immediately, with your favorite side dishes.

Vegan Thai Lettuce Wraps

🍴 4 servings   🕐 35 minutes

INGREDIENTS

For the Filling:
- 1 block (14 oz) firm tofu, pressed and crumbled
- 2 tablespoons olive oil
- 1 small onion, finely chopped
- 2 cloves garlic, minced
- 1 carrot, grated
- 1 red bell pepper, finely diced
- 1 cup mushrooms, finely chopped
- 1/2 cup cashews, roughly chopped
- 2 green onions, sliced
- 1/4 cup cilantro, chopped
- Salt and pepper, to taste

For the Sauce:
- 1/4 cup peanut butter
- 2 tablespoons soy sauce or tamari (for gluten-free)
- 1 tablespoon maple syrup or agave nectar
- 1 tablespoon lime juice
- 1 teaspoon chili garlic sauce or Sriracha (adjust to taste)
- 2-3 tablespoons warm water (to thin)

For Serving:
- Large lettuce leaves (such as Bibb or romaine)
- Extra lime wedges
- Additional chopped cilantro and sliced green onions

DIRECTIONS

1. **Prepare the Tofu:** In a large skillet, heat the olive oil over medium heat. Add the crumbled tofu and cook until browned, stirring occasionally, about 10 minutes. Transfer to a bowl.
2. **Cook the Vegetables:** In the same skillet, add a bit more oil if needed. Sauté the onion and garlic until soft, about 3 minutes. Add the carrot, red bell pepper, and mushrooms. Cook until the vegetables are tender, about 5 minutes. Season with salt and pepper.
3. **Combine Filling:** Return the cooked tofu to the skillet with the vegetables. Add the cashews, green onions, and cilantro. Stir to combine and cook for another 2 minutes. Adjust seasoning as needed.
4. **Make the Sauce:** In a small bowl, whisk together the peanut butter, soy sauce, maple syrup, lime juice, chili garlic sauce, and warm water until smooth. Adjust the thickness by adding more water if needed.
5. **Assemble the Lettuce Wraps:** Spoon the tofu-vegetable mixture into the center of each lettuce leaf. Drizzle with peanut sauce and garnish with additional cilantro and green onions.
6. **Serve:** Serve the lettuce wraps immediately with extra lime wedges on the side for squeezing.

Curried Vegan Potato Salad

🍴 6 servings   🕐 95 minutes

INGREDIENTS

- 2 lbs potatoes (Yukon gold or red potatoes work well), peeled and cut into bite-sized pieces
- 1 cup vegan mayonnaise
- 1 tablespoon curry powder
- 1 teaspoon turmeric
- 1/2 teaspoon garlic powder
- 1/2 teaspoon onion powder
- 2 tablespoons apple cider vinegar
- 1 tablespoon maple syrup or agave nectar
- Salt and pepper, to taste
- 1/2 cup red onion, finely chopped
- 1/2 cup celery, finely chopped
- 1/2 cup raisins or dried cranberries (optional)
- 1/4 cup fresh cilantro or parsley, chopped, plus more for garnish
- 1/4 cup slivered almonds or cashews (optional, for crunch)

DIRECTIONS

1. **Cook the Potatoes:** Place the potato pieces in a large pot and cover with cold water. Bring to a boil over medium-high heat, then reduce the heat to maintain a gentle boil. Cook until the potatoes are tender but not falling apart, about 10-15 minutes. Drain the potatoes and let them cool to room temperature.
2. **Make the Dressing:** In a large bowl, whisk together the vegan mayonnaise, curry powder, turmeric, garlic powder, onion powder, apple cider vinegar, and maple syrup. Season with salt and pepper to taste.
3. **Combine the Salad:** Add the cooled potatoes to the bowl with the dressing. Add the chopped red onion, celery, raisins (if using), and chopped cilantro or parsley. Gently toss until the potatoes are well coated with the dressing.
4. **Chill:** Cover and refrigerate the potato salad for at least 1 hour to allow the flavors to meld. This salad tastes best when chilled and the flavors have had time to develop.
5. **Serve:** Before serving, give the salad a gentle stir. Adjust seasoning if necessary. Garnish with additional fresh herbs and slivered almonds or cashews if desired.

Vegan Tuna Salad

 2-4 servings  45 minutes

INGREDIENTS

- 1 can (15 oz) chickpeas, drained and rinsed
- 1/4 cup vegan mayonnaise
- 1 tablespoon Dijon mustard
- 1 tablespoon apple cider vinegar
- 1 teaspoon kelp powder (optional, for a sea-like flavor)
- 1/2 cup celery, finely chopped
- 1/4 cup red onion, finely chopped
- 2 tablespoons dill pickles, finely chopped
- Salt and pepper, to taste
- Fresh lemon juice, to taste
- Fresh dill or parsley, chopped (optional, for garnish)

DIRECTIONS

1. **Mash the Chickpeas:** In a medium bowl, use a fork or potato masher to mash the chickpeas until they are broken down but still have some texture.
2. **Mix the Salad:** To the mashed chickpeas, add vegan mayonnaise, Dijon mustard, apple cider vinegar, and kelp powder if using. Stir until well combined. Mix in the chopped celery, red onion, and dill pickles. Season with salt, pepper, and a squeeze of fresh lemon juice to taste.
3. **Chill (Optional):** For the best flavor, cover and refrigerate the salad for at least 30 minutes to allow the flavors to meld together.
4. **Serve:** Serve the vegan tuna salad on bread or toast for a sandwich, wrap it in lettuce leaves for a low-carb option, or enjoy it as a dip with crackers. Garnish with fresh dill or parsley before serving.

Vegan Kimchi Quesadillas

 4 quesadillas  16 minutes

INGREDIENTS

- 4 large flour tortillas (use gluten-free if needed)
- 1 cup vegan cheese shreds (cheddar or mozzarella style works well)
- 1 cup vegan kimchi, roughly chopped (ensure it's vegan, as some kimchi contains fish sauce)
- 1/2 cup black beans, rinsed and drained (optional)
- 2 green onions, sliced
- 1 tablespoon vegetable oil, for cooking
- Vegan sour cream, for serving (optional)
- Sriracha or hot sauce, for serving (optional)

DIRECTIONS

1. **Prepare the Filling:** In a medium bowl, mix together the chopped kimchi, black beans (if using), and sliced green onions.
2. **Assemble the Quesadillas:** Lay out the tortillas on a flat surface. Sprinkle half of each tortilla with vegan cheese shreds. Top the cheese with an even layer of the kimchi mixture. Fold the tortillas in half over the filling to create a half-moon shape.
3. **Cook the Quesadillas:** Heat a skillet or griddle over medium heat and brush with a little vegetable oil. Place the quesadillas in the skillet, cooking in batches if necessary, and cook for 2-3 minutes on each side until the tortillas are golden brown and crispy, and the cheese has melted. Press down gently on the quesadillas with a spatula while cooking to ensure even heating.
4. **Serve:** Cut the quesadillas into wedges and serve hot with vegan sour cream and sriracha or hot sauce on the side for dipping.

Vegan Pita Pockets with Roasted Veggies

 4 servings    40 minutes

INGREDIENTS

For the Roasted Veggies:

- 1 red bell pepper, sliced
- 1 yellow bell pepper, sliced
- 1 zucchini, sliced
- 1 red onion, sliced
- 1 cup cherry tomatoes, halved
- 2 tablespoons olive oil
- 1 teaspoon dried oregano
- Salt and pepper, to taste

For the Tahini Sauce:

- 1/4 cup tahini
- 2 tablespoons lemon juice
- 1 clove garlic, minced
- 2-4 tablespoons water (to thin)
- Salt, to taste

Additional Ingredients:

- 4 pita bread pockets
- Fresh spinach or mixed greens
- Fresh parsley or cilantro, chopped (for garnish)

DIRECTIONS

1. **Roast the Veggies:** Preheat your oven to 425°F (220°C). Line a baking sheet with parchment paper. In a large bowl, toss the sliced bell peppers, zucchini, red onion, and cherry tomatoes with olive oil, oregano, salt, and pepper until well coated. Spread the vegetables in a single layer on the prepared baking sheet. Roast in the oven for 20-25 minutes, or until tender and slightly charred. Stir halfway through cooking.

2. **Prepare the Tahini Sauce:** In a small bowl, whisk together tahini, lemon juice, minced garlic, and salt. Gradually add water, one tablespoon at a time, until the sauce reaches a pourable consistency.

3. **Assemble the Pita Pockets:** If desired, lightly toast the pita bread. Carefully open each pita pocket to create a space for the fillings. Start with a layer of fresh spinach or mixed greens inside each pita pocket. Spoon a generous amount of the roasted vegetables into each pita. Drizzle with the tahini sauce and garnish with chopped parsley or cilantro.

4. **Serve:** Serve the Vegan Pita Pockets immediately, with extra tahini sauce on the side for dipping if desired.

Lentil and Avocado Salad

 4 servings    40 minutes

INGREDIENTS

- 1 cup dried green or brown lentils, rinsed
- 2 ripe avocados, pitted and diced
- 1 large tomato, diced
- 1/2 red onion, finely chopped
- 1/2 cucumber, diced
- 1/4 cup fresh parsley or cilantro, chopped
- Juice of 1 lemon
- 2 tablespoons olive oil
- 1 tablespoon apple cider vinegar
- 1 garlic clove, minced
- Salt and pepper, to taste
- Optional: crumbled vegan feta cheese, for garnish

DIRECTIONS

1. **Cook the Lentils:** In a medium saucepan, bring 3 cups of water to a boil. Add the lentils, reduce the heat to low, cover, and simmer for 20-25 minutes, or until the lentils are tender but still hold their shape. Drain any excess water and let the lentils cool to room temperature.
2. **Prepare the Dressing:** In a small bowl, whisk together lemon juice, olive oil, apple cider vinegar, minced garlic, salt, and pepper. Adjust the seasoning according to taste.
3. **Assemble the Salad:** In a large bowl, combine the cooled lentils, diced avocados, tomatoes, red onion, cucumber, and parsley or cilantro. Gently toss to combine.
4. **Dress the Salad:** Pour the dressing over the salad and gently toss to ensure all the ingredients are well coated.
5. **Serve:** Serve the salad immediately, garnished with crumbled vegan feta cheese if desired.

Vegan Jerk Tofu Wraps

 4 wraps    30 minutes

INGREDIENTS

For the Jerk Tofu:
- 1 block (14 oz) extra-firm tofu, pressed and sliced into strips
- 3 tablespoons jerk seasoning paste (ensure it's vegan-friendly)
- 2 tablespoons soy sauce or tamari (for gluten-free option)
- 1 tablespoon vegetable oil

For the Creamy Sauce:
- 1/2 cup vegan mayonnaise
- 1 tablespoon lime juice
- 1 teaspoon agave syrup or maple syrup
- 1/2 teaspoon garlic powder
- Salt to taste

For the Wrap:
- 4 large flour tortillas (use gluten-free if needed)
- 2 cups mixed salad greens
- 1 ripe avocado, sliced
- 1 red bell pepper, thinly sliced
- 1/2 cucumber, thinly sliced
- 1/4 red onion, thinly sliced

DIRECTIONS

1. **Marinate the Tofu:** In a bowl, mix the jerk seasoning paste and soy sauce. Add the tofu strips, ensuring they're well coated with the marinade. Let sit for at least 30 minutes, or for better flavor, marinate in the refrigerator overnight.
2. **Cook the Tofu:** Heat vegetable oil in a skillet over medium-high heat. Add the marinated tofu strips and cook until browned and crispy on all sides, about 5-7 minutes per side. Set aside.
3. **Prepare the Creamy Sauce:** In a small bowl, whisk together vegan mayonnaise, lime juice, agave syrup, garlic powder, and salt until smooth. Adjust the seasoning to taste.
4. **Assemble the Wraps:** Warm the tortillas in a skillet or microwave. Lay out each tortilla on a flat surface. Spread a layer of the creamy sauce over each tortilla. Then, arrange a bed of mixed salad greens in the center. Top the greens with slices of cooked jerk tofu, avocado, red bell pepper, cucumber, and red onion.
5. **Roll the Wraps:** Carefully fold in the sides of the tortilla, then roll it up tightly from the bottom to enclose the fillings.
6. **Serve:** Cut each wrap in half diagonally and serve immediately, with extra creamy sauce on the side if desired.

Vegan Miso Soup with Noodles and Vegetables

🍴 4 servings　🕐 35 minutes

INGREDIENTS

- 4 cups vegetable broth
- 2 cups water
- 3 tablespoons miso paste (white or red, ensure it's vegan)
- 2 teaspoons soy sauce or tamari (for gluten-free option)
- 8 oz noodles (soba, udon, or rice noodles work well)
- 1 block (14 oz) firm tofu, cubed
- 1 cup mushrooms (shiitake, cremini, or button), sliced
- 1 cup spinach or kale, roughly chopped
- 1/2 cup carrots, julienned
- 1/2 cup green onions, sliced
- 1 sheet nori (seaweed), cut into strips (optional)
- 1 tablespoon sesame oil (for sautéing)
- Salt and pepper, to taste

DIRECTIONS

1. **Prepare the Noodles:** Cook the noodles according to the package instructions. Drain, rinse with cold water to stop the cooking process, and set aside.
2. **Sauté the Vegetables:** In a large pot, heat the sesame oil over medium heat. Add the mushrooms and carrots, sautéing until they start to soften, about 5 minutes. Add the green onions (save some for garnish) and cook for an additional 2 minutes.
3. **Simmer the Broth:** Add the vegetable broth and water to the pot. Bring to a simmer over medium heat.
4. **Dissolve the Miso Paste:** In a small bowl, mix the miso paste with a little hot broth from the pot until smooth. This prevents clumps. Stir the miso mixture back into the pot.
5. **Add the Tofu and Greens:** Add the cubed tofu and chopped spinach or kale to the pot. Simmer gently for 3–5 minutes, or until the greens are wilted and the tofu is heated through. Avoid boiling to preserve the miso's flavor and probiotics.
6. **Combine Noodles and Soup:** Divide the cooked noodles among serving bowls. Ladle the hot miso soup with vegetables and tofu over the noodles.
7. **Serve:** Garnish each bowl with nori strips and the reserved sliced green onions. Season with salt and pepper to taste.

Vegan Caesar Salad with Tempeh Croutons

 4 servings  40 minutes

INGREDIENTS

For the Tempeh Croutons:

- 8 oz tempeh, cut into small cubes
- 2 tablespoons soy sauce or tamari (for gluten-free option)
- 1 tablespoon olive oil
- 1 teaspoon garlic powder
- 1/2 teaspoon smoked paprika

For the Vegan Caesar Dressing:

- 1/2 cup raw cashews, soaked for 4 hours or overnight and drained
- 1/4 cup water
- 2 tablespoons lemon juice
- 1 tablespoon olive oil
- 1 tablespoon capers
- 1 clove garlic
- 2 teaspoons Dijon mustard
- 1 teaspoon nutritional yeast
- Salt and black pepper, to taste

For the Salad:

- 2 heads romaine lettuce, chopped
- 1/4 cup vegan Parmesan cheese (optional)
- Additional lemon wedges, for serving

DIRECTIONS

1. **Prepare the Tempeh Croutons:** Preheat your oven to 375°F (190°C). Line a baking sheet with parchment paper. In a bowl, combine the tempeh cubes with soy sauce, olive oil, garlic powder, and smoked paprika. Toss until the tempeh is evenly coated. Spread the tempeh cubes on the prepared baking sheet in a single layer. Bake for 20-25 minutes, or until the tempeh is crispy and golden. Stir halfway through baking.

2. **Make the Vegan Caesar Dressing:** In a blender, combine the soaked and drained cashews, water, lemon juice, olive oil, capers, garlic, Dijon mustard, nutritional yeast, salt, and pepper. Blend until smooth and creamy. Adjust the seasoning and consistency by adding more water, if needed.

3. **Assemble the Salad:** In a large salad bowl, toss the chopped romaine lettuce with the vegan Caesar dressing until well coated. Add more or less dressing to your preference.

4. **Serve:** Top the dressed salad with the baked tempeh croutons and vegan Parmesan cheese, if using. Serve with additional lemon wedges on the side.

Roasted Vegetable and Hummus Tartines

☆☆☆☆☆

🍴 4 tartines   🕐 35 minutes

INGREDIENTS

- Assorted vegetables for roasting (e.g., bell peppers, zucchini, eggplant, cherry tomatoes), sliced or chopped
- 2 tablespoons olive oil
- Salt and pepper, to taste
- 4 slices of rustic bread or sourdough
- 1 cup hummus (store-bought or homemade)
- Fresh herbs (such as basil, parsley, or thyme) for garnish
- Optional toppings: sliced avocado, pumpkin seeds, sprouts, or a drizzle of balsamic glaze

DIRECTIONS

1. **Roast the Vegetables:** Preheat your oven to 425°F (220°C). Line a baking sheet with parchment paper. Toss the sliced vegetables with olive oil, salt, and pepper. Spread them out on the prepared baking sheet in a single layer. Roast in the oven for 20-25 minutes, or until the vegetables are tender and have caramelized edges. Flip or stir halfway through cooking for even roasting.
2. **Toast the Bread:** While the vegetables are roasting, toast the slices of bread until golden and crisp. You can use a toaster or place them in the oven on a separate rack for the last 5-10 minutes of the vegetables' cooking time.
3. **Assemble the Tartines:** Spread a generous layer of hummus on each slice of toasted bread. Top with the roasted vegetables, arranging them in an even layer.
4. **Garnish and Serve:** Garnish the tartines with fresh herbs and any optional toppings you like, such as sliced avocado, pumpkin seeds, sprouts, or a drizzle of balsamic glaze. Serve immediately while the vegetables are still warm, or at room temperature.

Vegan BBQ Pulled Porcini Sandwiches

4-6 sandwiches   55 minutes

INGREDIENTS

- 2 cups dried porcini mushrooms
- Boiling water, enough to cover the mushrooms
- 1 tablespoon olive oil
- 1 small onion, finely chopped
- 2 cloves garlic, minced
- 1 cup vegan barbecue sauce (store-bought or homemade)
- Salt and pepper, to taste
- 4-6 vegan burger buns
- Optional toppings: coleslaw, pickles, sliced avocado, vegan cheese slices

DIRECTIONS

1. **Rehydrate the Porcini Mushrooms:** Place the dried porcini mushrooms in a large bowl. Cover them with boiling water and let soak for 20-30 minutes, or until they are soft and pliable. Drain the mushrooms and gently squeeze out the excess water. Pull apart or chop the mushrooms into smaller pieces to mimic pulled pork texture.

2. **Cook the Mushrooms:** Heat the olive oil in a large skillet over medium heat. Add the chopped onion and garlic, sautéing until soft and translucent, about 5 minutes. Add the rehydrated porcini mushrooms to the skillet. Cook, stirring occasionally, until the mushrooms start to brown and crisp up slightly, about 8-10 minutes.

3. **Add BBQ Sauce:** Pour the vegan barbecue sauce over the mushrooms in the skillet. Reduce the heat to low and simmer for 10-15 minutes, or until the sauce has thickened and the mushrooms are well coated. Season with salt and pepper to taste.

4. **Prepare the Sandwiches:** Toast the vegan burger buns if desired. Spoon a generous amount of the BBQ pulled porcini mixture onto the bottom halves of the buns.

5. **Add Toppings and Serve:** If using, add your choice of optional toppings such as coleslaw, pickles, sliced avocado, or vegan cheese. Place the top half of the bun on each sandwich. Serve the sandwiches hot, with extra barbecue sauce on the side if desired.

# Spicy Chickpea and Quinoa Bowl

🍴 4 servings 🕐 45 minutes

INGREDIENTS

- 1 cup quinoa, rinsed
- 2 cups vegetable broth or water
- 1 can (15 oz) chickpeas, drained, rinsed, and dried
- 1 tablespoon olive oil
- 1 teaspoon smoked paprika
- 1/2 teaspoon ground cumin
- 1/4 teaspoon cayenne pepper (adjust according to spice preference)
- Salt and pepper, to taste
- 1 avocado, sliced
- 1 cup cherry tomatoes, halved
- 1/2 cucumber, diced
- 1/4 red onion, thinly sliced
- Fresh cilantro or parsley, chopped (for garnish)
- Lemon wedges, for serving

For the Dressing:
- 1/4 cup tahini
- 2 tablespoons lemon juice
- 1 clove garlic, minced
- 2-4 tablespoons water (to thin)
- Salt, to taste

DIRECTIONS

1. **Cook the Quinoa:** In a medium saucepan, bring the vegetable broth or water to a boil. Add the quinoa, reduce heat to low, cover, and simmer for 15-20 minutes, or until the liquid is absorbed and the quinoa is fluffy. Remove from heat and let it stand covered for 5 minutes. Fluff with a fork.
2. **Roast the Chickpeas:** Preheat your oven to 425°F (220°C). Toss the chickpeas with olive oil, smoked paprika, cumin, cayenne pepper, salt, and pepper. Spread them on a baking sheet in a single layer. Roast for 20-25 minutes, or until crispy, shaking the pan halfway through.
3. **Prepare the Dressing:** In a small bowl, whisk together tahini, lemon juice, minced garlic, and salt. Gradually add water until the dressing reaches a pourable consistency.
4. **Assemble the Bowls:** Divide the cooked quinoa among bowls. Top with roasted chickpeas, sliced avocado, cherry tomatoes, diced cucumber, and red onion.
5. **Serve:** Drizzle the tahini dressing over each bowl. Garnish with chopped cilantro or parsley and serve with lemon wedges on the side.

Vegan Soba Noodle Salad

 4 servings    25 minutes

INGREDIENTS

- 8 oz soba noodles
- 1 red bell pepper, thinly sliced
- 1 carrot, julienned or grated
- 1 cucumber, julienned or sliced into thin rounds
- 3 green onions, thinly sliced
- 1/4 cup cilantro, chopped
- 1 tablespoon sesame seeds, toasted (for garnish)

For the Dressing:
- 3 tablespoons soy sauce or tamari (for a gluten-free option)
- 2 tablespoons rice vinegar
- 1 tablespoon sesame oil
- 1 tablespoon lime juice
- 2 teaspoons maple syrup or agave nectar
- 1 clove garlic, minced
- 1 teaspoon ginger, grated
- 1 teaspoon chili flakes (adjust according to spice preference)

DIRECTIONS

1. **Cook the Soba Noodles:** Cook the soba noodles according to the package instructions. Be careful not to overcook; they should be al dente. Rinse under cold water to stop the cooking process and drain well.
2. **Prepare the Vegetables:** While the noodles are cooking, prepare the red bell pepper, carrot, cucumber, green onions, and cilantro as described.
3. **Make the Dressing:** In a small bowl, whisk together the soy sauce, rice vinegar, sesame oil, lime juice, maple syrup, minced garlic, grated ginger, and chili flakes until well combined.
4. **Combine and Toss:** In a large mixing bowl, combine the cooked and cooled soba noodles with the prepared vegetables. Pour the dressing over the noodle and vegetable mixture, tossing until everything is evenly coated.
5. **Serve:** Transfer the noodle salad to serving plates or a large serving dish. Garnish with toasted sesame seeds and additional cilantro if desired. This salad can be served immediately or chilled in the refrigerator for 1 hour before serving for a cooler, more refreshing dish.

Vegan Falafel Bowl with Tahini Dressing

 4 servings    50 minutes

INGREDIENTS

For the Falafel:

- 1 can (15 oz) chickpeas, drained and rinsed
- 1/4 cup fresh parsley, roughly chopped
- 1/4 cup fresh cilantro, roughly chopped
- 3 cloves garlic, minced
- 1 small onion, chopped
- 2 tablespoons flour (use chickpea flour for gluten-free option)
- 1 teaspoon ground cumin
- 1 teaspoon ground coriander
- Salt and pepper, to taste
- Oil for frying or baking

For the Bowl:

- 2 cups cooked quinoa or rice
- 1 cucumber, diced
- 1 tomato, diced
- 1/2 red onion, thinly sliced
- 1 cup mixed greens (spinach, arugula, lettuce)
- 1/4 cup Kalamata olives, pitted
- 1/4 cup pickled turnips or radishes (optional)

For the Tahini Dressing:

- 1/3 cup tahini
- 2 tablespoons lemon juice
- 1 clove garlic, minced
- Water, as needed to thin
- Salt, to taste

DIRECTIONS

1. **Make the Falafel:** In a food processor, combine chickpeas, parsley, cilantro, garlic, onion, flour, cumin, coriander, salt, and pepper. Pulse until well mixed but not pureed. Form the mixture into small balls or patties. If the mixture is too wet, you may add a little more flour. For baking, preheat the oven to 375°F (190°C), place falafel on a greased baking sheet, and bake for 25-30 minutes, flipping halfway through, until golden and crispy. For frying, heat oil in a pan over medium heat and fry the falafel until golden brown on all sides.

2. **Prepare the Tahini Dressing:** Whisk together tahini, lemon juice, minced garlic, and salt in a bowl. Gradually add water until you achieve a pourable consistency.

3. **Assemble the Bowl:** Divide the cooked quinoa or rice among serving bowls. Arrange the cucumber, tomato, red onion, mixed greens, olives, and pickled turnips (if using) around the bowl. Top with falafel.

4. **Serve:** Drizzle the tahini dressing over each bowl before serving. Garnish with additional parsley or cilantro if desired.

Dinner

Vegan Mushroom Stroganoff

🍴 4 servings   🕐 30 minutes

INGREDIENTS

For the Vegan Mushroom Stroganoff:

- 1 pound (450g) mushrooms (such as cremini or white button), sliced
- 1 large onion, finely chopped
- 2 cloves garlic, minced
- 2 tablespoons olive oil
- 1 tablespoon soy sauce or tamari (for gluten-free option)
- 2 tablespoons all-purpose flour (use gluten-free flour if needed)
- 2 cups vegetable broth
- 1 cup vegan sour cream (or use a blend of soaked cashews and water for a homemade version)
- Salt and pepper, to taste
- 1 teaspoon smoked paprika (optional for a smoky flavor)
- Fresh parsley, chopped, for garnish

For Serving:

- 8 oz (about 225g) pasta (such as fettuccine, linguine, or a gluten-free alternative), cooked according to package instructions
- Or cooked rice, for a gluten-free option

DIRECTIONS

1. **Cook the Mushrooms and Onions:** In a large skillet or saucepan, heat the olive oil over medium heat. Add the onions and garlic, sautéing until the onions become translucent and soft, about 5 minutes. Add the sliced mushrooms and soy sauce, and continue to cook, stirring occasionally, until the mushrooms have released their moisture and become golden brown, about 10 minutes.

2. **Make the Stroganoff Sauce:** Sprinkle the flour over the mushrooms and onions, stirring to coat them evenly. Cook for a minute to remove the raw flour taste. Gradually add the vegetable broth, stirring constantly to incorporate and prevent lumps from forming. Bring the mixture to a simmer. Reduce the heat to low and stir in the vegan sour cream. Season with salt, pepper, and smoked paprika (if using). Continue to cook, stirring occasionally, until the sauce thickens, about 5 minutes. Adjust the seasoning as needed.

3. **Serve:** Serve the mushroom stroganoff over cooked pasta or rice. Garnish with fresh chopped parsley.

Lentil Bolognese with Spaghetti

 4 servings    1 hour

INGREDIENTS

For the Lentil Bolognese:

- 1 cup dried green or brown lentils, rinsed
- 2 tablespoons olive oil
- 1 large onion, finely chopped
- 2 carrots, peeled and finely chopped
- 2 celery stalks, finely chopped
- 3 garlic cloves, minced
- 1 can (28 oz) crushed tomatoes
- 2 tablespoons tomato paste
- 1 cup vegetable broth
- 1 teaspoon dried oregano
- 1 teaspoon dried basil
- 1/2 teaspoon red pepper flakes (optional, for heat)
- Salt and pepper, to taste
- Fresh basil, for garnish

For Serving:

- 8 oz (225g) spaghetti (use whole wheat or gluten-free if preferred), cooked according to package instructions

DIRECTIONS

1. **Cook the Lentils:** In a medium saucepan, combine the lentils with enough water to cover them by a couple of inches. Bring to a boil, then reduce the heat to low, cover, and simmer for about 20-25 minutes, or until the lentils are tender but not mushy. Drain any excess water and set aside.

2. **Prepare the Bolognese Sauce:** While the lentils are cooking, heat the olive oil in a large skillet or saucepan over medium heat. Add the onion, carrots, and celery. Cook, stirring occasionally, until the vegetables are softened, about 5-7 minutes. Add the minced garlic and cook for another minute, until fragrant. Stir in the crushed tomatoes, tomato paste, cooked lentils, vegetable broth, oregano, dried basil, red pepper flakes (if using), salt, and pepper. Bring to a simmer. Reduce the heat to low and let the sauce simmer, partially covered, for about 30 minutes, stirring occasionally. If the sauce becomes too thick, add a little more vegetable broth to reach your desired consistency.

3. **Serve:** Taste the Bolognese sauce and adjust the seasoning with more salt and pepper if needed. Serve the lentil Bolognese over cooked spaghetti. Garnish with fresh basil leaves.

Vegan Meatloaf

 6-8 servings  1,5 hours

INGREDIENTS

For the Vegan Meatloaf:

- 1 cup dried green lentils, rinsed
- 2 1/2 cups vegetable broth
- 1 bay leaf
- 1 tablespoon olive oil
- 1 small onion, finely chopped
- 2 cloves garlic, minced
- 1 cup cremini or white mushrooms, finely chopped
- 1 carrot, grated
- 1/2 cup walnuts, finely ground
- 1/2 cup quick oats (gluten-free if necessary)
- 1/2 cup breadcrumbs (use gluten-free breadcrumbs if needed)
- 2 tablespoons soy sauce or tamari (for a gluten-free option)
- 2 tablespoons tomato paste
- 1 tablespoon ground flaxseed mixed with 3 tablespoons water (flax egg)
- 1 teaspoon smoked paprika
- 1 teaspoon dried thyme
- Salt and pepper, to taste

For the Glaze:

- 1/2 cup ketchup
- 1 tablespoon apple cider vinegar
- 2 tablespoons brown sugar or maple syrup
- 1 teaspoon smoked paprika

DIRECTIONS

1. **Cook the Lentils:** In a medium saucepan, combine the lentils, vegetable broth, and bay leaf. Bring to a boil, then reduce heat, cover, and simmer for about 25-30 minutes, or until the lentils are tender but not mushy. Drain any excess liquid and remove the bay leaf.

2. **Sauté the Vegetables:** While the lentils are cooking, heat the olive oil in a skillet over medium heat. Add the onion and garlic, and sauté until softened, about 5 minutes. Add the mushrooms and carrot, and continue to cook until the vegetables are tender and the mushrooms have released their moisture, about 5-7 more minutes. Set aside to cool slightly.

3. **Prepare the Meatloaf Mixture:** Preheat your oven to 375°F (190°C) and line a loaf pan with parchment paper. In a large bowl, mash half of the cooked lentils. Add the remaining whole lentils, sautéed vegetable mixture, ground walnuts, oats, breadcrumbs, soy sauce, tomato paste, flax egg, smoked paprika, thyme, salt, and pepper. Mix until well combined.

4. **Shape and Bake:** Transfer the mixture to the prepared loaf pan, pressing it down firmly and shaping the top smoothly with a spatula or your hands. In a small bowl, mix together all the ingredients for the glaze. Spread the glaze evenly over the top of the meatloaf. Bake in the preheated oven for about 40-45 minutes, or until the meatloaf is firm and the glaze is caramelized.

5. **Serve:** Let the vegan meatloaf cool in the pan for about 10 minutes before lifting it out using the parchment paper. Slice and serve warm.

Stuffed Acorn Squash

 4 servings    1 hour

INGREDIENTS

For the Squash:

- 2 acorn squashes, halved and seeds removed
- 2 tablespoons olive oil
- Salt and pepper, to taste

For the Filling:

- 1 tablespoon olive oil
- 1 small onion, diced
- 2 cloves garlic, minced
- 1 cup mushrooms, chopped (optional)
- 1 cup quinoa, rinsed
- 2 cups vegetable broth
- 1 teaspoon dried thyme
- 1/2 teaspoon dried sage
- 1/2 cup dried cranberries
- 1/2 cup pecans, chopped and toasted
- 1/4 cup fresh parsley, chopped
- Salt and pepper, to taste

DIRECTIONS

1. **Roast the Squash:** Preheat your oven to 400°F (200°C). Line a baking sheet with parchment paper. Brush the cut sides of the acorn squash with olive oil and season with salt and pepper. Place the squash halves cut-side down on the prepared baking sheet. Roast for about 25-30 minutes, or until the flesh is tender when pierced with a fork.
2. **Cook the Quinoa:** While the squash is roasting, heat 1 tablespoon of olive oil in a medium saucepan over medium heat. Add the diced onion and cook until translucent, about 5 minutes. Add the garlic (and mushrooms if using) and cook for another 2-3 minutes. Stir in the quinoa, vegetable broth, thyme, and sage. Bring to a boil, then reduce heat to low, cover, and simmer for about 15 minutes, or until the liquid is absorbed and the quinoa is fluffy.
3. **Prepare the Filling:** Once the quinoa is cooked, remove it from heat. Stir in the dried cranberries, toasted pecans, and fresh parsley. Season with salt and pepper to taste.
4. **Stuff the Squash:** Turn the roasted acorn squash halves cut-side up on the baking sheet. Divide the quinoa filling among the squash halves, gently packing it in.
5. **Final Roast:** Return the stuffed squash to the oven and roast for another 10-15 minutes, or until everything is heated through and the tops are slightly golden.
6. **Serve:** Serve the stuffed acorn squash warm, garnished with additional parsley if desired.

Vegan Shepherd's Pie

 6-8 servings    1 hour 15 minutes

INGREDIENTS

For the Lentil-Vegetable Filling:

- 1 tablespoon olive oil
- 1 large onion, diced
- 2 cloves garlic, minced
- 2 carrots, peeled and diced
- 2 stalks celery, diced
- 8 oz (about 225g) mushrooms, chopped
- 1 cup dried green or brown lentils, rinsed
- 3 cups vegetable broth
- 1 tablespoon tomato paste
- 1 teaspoon dried thyme
- 1 teaspoon dried rosemary
- Salt and pepper, to taste
- 1 cup frozen peas
- 1 cup corn kernels (fresh, frozen, or canned and drained)

For the Mashed Potato Topping:

- 2 lbs (about 900g) potatoes, peeled and chopped
- 1/4 cup vegan butter
- 1/4 cup unsweetened plant-based milk
- Salt and pepper, to taste

DIRECTIONS

1. **Preheat the Oven:** Preheat your oven to 375°F (190°C).
2. **Cook the Lentil-Vegetable Filling:** Heat the olive oil in a large pan over medium heat. Add the onion, garlic, carrots, and celery, and sauté until the vegetables start to soften, about 5 minutes. Add the chopped mushrooms and cook until they release their moisture and begin to brown, about 5-7 minutes. Stir in the lentils, vegetable broth, tomato paste, thyme, rosemary, salt, and pepper. Bring the mixture to a boil, then reduce the heat and simmer, covered, for about 25-30 minutes, or until the lentils are tender. Add the frozen peas and corn to the pan, and cook for an additional 5 minutes. Adjust seasoning if necessary. Spread the lentil-vegetable mixture in an even layer in a large baking dish.
3. **Prepare the Mashed Potato Topping:** While the filling is cooking, boil the chopped potatoes in a large pot of salted water until tender, about 15-20 minutes. Drain the potatoes and return them to the pot. Add the vegan butter, plant-based milk, salt, and pepper. Mash until smooth and creamy. Adjust seasoning to taste.
4. **Assemble and Bake:** Spread the mashed potatoes over the lentil-vegetable filling in the baking dish. Use a fork to create ridges on top if desired. Bake in the preheated oven for 20-25 minutes, or until the top is golden and the edges are bubbling.
5. **Serve:** Let the vegan shepherd's pie cool for a few minutes before serving. Garnish with fresh herbs if desired.

Eggplant Parmesan (Vegan)

☆☆☆☆☆

🍴 4-6 servings 🕐 1 hour 15 minutes

INGREDIENTS

For the Eggplant:

- 2 medium eggplants, sliced into 1/2-inch thick rounds
- Salt, for drawing out moisture from eggplant
- 1 cup all-purpose flour (or gluten-free alternative)
- 1 cup unsweetened plant-based milk
- 1 tablespoon apple cider vinegar
- 2 cups breadcrumbs (use gluten-free if needed)
- 1 teaspoon Italian seasoning
- 1/2 teaspoon garlic powder
- 1/2 teaspoon salt
- Olive oil or cooking spray, for baking

For the Assembly:

- 2 cups marinara sauce
- 2 cups vegan mozzarella cheese, shredded
- 1/4 cup vegan parmesan cheese, grated
- Fresh basil leaves, for garnish

DIRECTIONS

1. **Prep the Eggplant:** Sprinkle salt on both sides of the eggplant slices and lay them on paper towels for about 30 minutes to draw out moisture. Rinse with water and pat dry.
2. **Preheat the Oven and Prepare Baking Sheets:** Preheat your oven to 400°F (200°C). Line two large baking sheets with parchment paper and lightly grease with olive oil or cooking spray.
3. **Batter and Breading:** Set up a breading station with three shallow dishes: one with flour, one with plant-based milk mixed with apple cider vinegar (to create a vegan "buttermilk"), and one with breadcrumbs mixed with Italian seasoning, garlic powder, and salt. Dredge each eggplant slice in flour, dip in the milk mixture, then coat with the breadcrumb mixture. Place on the prepared baking sheets in a single layer.
4. **Bake the Eggplant:** Bake the breaded eggplant slices for 20-25 minutes, flipping halfway through, until they are golden brown and crispy. Remove from oven.
5. **Assemble the Eggplant Parmesan:** In a baking dish, spread a thin layer of marinara sauce. Arrange a layer of baked eggplant slices over the sauce. Top with a generous amount of marinara sauce, then sprinkle with vegan mozzarella cheese. Repeat the layers until all ingredients are used, finishing with a layer of cheese.
6. **Bake:** Bake in the preheated oven for 20-25 minutes, or until the cheese is melted and bubbly. For a golden top, broil for the last few minutes, watching carefully to avoid burning.
7. **Serve:** Garnish with vegan parmesan cheese and fresh basil leaves. Serve hot with additional marinara sauce on the side, if desired.

Vegan Paella

 4-6 servings    50 minutes

INGREDIENTS

- 2 tablespoons olive oil
- 1 large onion, diced
- 3 cloves garlic, minced
- 1 red bell pepper, sliced
- 1 yellow bell pepper, sliced
- 1 cup green beans, trimmed and cut into 2-inch pieces
- 1 cup artichoke hearts, quartered (canned or frozen and thawed)
- 1 cup frozen peas, thawed
- 2 large tomatoes, diced
- 1 1/2 cups paella rice (short grain rice like Arborio or Bomba)
- 4 cups vegetable broth
- 1 teaspoon saffron threads, crushed (soaked in 1/4 cup warm water)
- 1 teaspoon smoked paprika
- 1/2 teaspoon turmeric (for color)
- Salt and pepper, to taste
- Lemon wedges, for serving
- Fresh parsley, chopped, for garnish

DIRECTIONS

1. **Prep and Cook the Vegetables:** In a large paella pan or a large, deep skillet, heat the olive oil over medium heat. Add the onion and garlic, and sauté until the onion is translucent. Add the sliced bell peppers and green beans, and cook for another 5-7 minutes, or until the vegetables start to soften. Stir in the artichoke hearts, peas, and tomatoes. Cook for another few minutes until the tomatoes release their juices.

2. **Add Rice and Spices:** Stir in the paella rice, making sure it's well-coated with the vegetable mixture. Add the vegetable broth, saffron (along with its soaking water), smoked paprika, turmeric, salt, and pepper. Stir to combine all the ingredients evenly.

3. **Cook the Paella:** Bring the mixture to a boil, then reduce the heat to low. Cover and simmer for about 20-25 minutes, or until the rice is cooked through and has absorbed the liquid. Avoid stirring the rice as it cooks to achieve the desired "socarrat" (a slightly crispy bottom).

4. **Final Touches:** Once the rice is cooked, remove the pan from heat and let it sit, covered, for 10 minutes to allow the flavors to meld.

5. **Serve:** Serve the paella warm, garnished with lemon wedges and a sprinkle of fresh parsley. Encourage guests to squeeze the lemon over their servings for added zest.

Vegan Thai Green Curry

 4 servings  40 minutes

INGREDIENTS

For the Vegan Thai Green Curry:

- 2 tablespoons coconut oil
- 2-3 tablespoons green curry paste (adjust according to taste and the brand's spice level)
- 1 can (14 oz) coconut milk
- 1 cup vegetable broth
- 1 tablespoon soy sauce or tamari (for a gluten-free option)
- 1 tablespoon maple syrup or sugar
- 1 bell pepper, sliced
- 1 zucchini, sliced into half-moons
- 1 cup broccoli florets
- 1 cup snap peas or green beans
- 1/2 cup bamboo shoots, optional
- 1 block (14 oz) firm tofu, pressed and cubed
- Salt to taste
- Fresh basil or cilantro leaves, for garnish
- Lime wedges, for serving

For Serving:

- Cooked jasmine or basmati rice

DIRECTIONS

1. **Prepare the Tofu:** Press the tofu to remove excess water and cut it into bite-sized cubes. Optionally, pan-fry the tofu cubes in a bit of coconut oil until golden brown on all sides for added texture. Set aside.
2. **Cook the Curry:** In a large skillet or wok, heat the coconut oil over medium heat. Add the green curry paste and sauté for 1-2 minutes, or until fragrant. Slowly pour in the coconut milk and vegetable broth, stirring until the curry paste is well blended with the liquids. Add the soy sauce and maple syrup, stirring to combine. Bring the mixture to a simmer.
3. **Add the Vegetables:** Add the sliced bell pepper, zucchini, broccoli, and snap peas to the skillet. If using, add the bamboo shoots as well. Let the curry simmer for about 10 minutes, or until the vegetables are tender but still crisp.
4. **Include the Tofu:** Gently stir in the tofu cubes, and cook for an additional 5 minutes, allowing the tofu to absorb the flavors of the curry. Taste and adjust seasoning with salt if necessary.
5. **Serve:** Serve the curry hot over cooked rice. Garnish with fresh basil or cilantro leaves and provide lime wedges on the side for squeezing.

Vegan Jambalaya

 4-6 servings  45 minutes

INGREDIENTS

- 2 tablespoons olive oil
- 1 large onion, diced
- 3 cloves garlic, minced
- 1 bell pepper (any color), diced
- 2 stalks celery, diced
- 1 large carrot, diced
- 1 zucchini, diced
- 1 cup okra, sliced (fresh or frozen)
- 1 can (14 oz) diced tomatoes, undrained
- 1 can (15 oz) red kidney beans, drained and rinsed
- 1 cup long-grain white rice
- 3 cups vegetable broth
- 2 teaspoons smoked paprika
- 1 teaspoon dried oregano
- 1 teaspoon dried thyme
- 1/2 teaspoon cayenne pepper (adjust to taste)
- Salt and black pepper, to taste
- 2 bay leaves
- Optional: 1 cup vegan sausage, sliced (such as andouille-style or your favorite vegan sausage)
- Fresh parsley, chopped, for garnish
- Green onions, sliced, for garnish

DIRECTIONS

1. **Sauté the Vegetables:** In a large pot or Dutch oven, heat the olive oil over medium heat. Add the onion, garlic, bell pepper, celery, and carrot. Sauté until the vegetables are softened, about 5-7 minutes. Add the zucchini and okra, and cook for an additional 3-4 minutes, until they begin to soften.

2. **Add the Main Ingredients:** Stir in the diced tomatoes (with their juices), kidney beans, rice, vegetable broth, smoked paprika, oregano, thyme, cayenne pepper, salt, and black pepper. Add the bay leaves and vegan sausage slices if using.

3. **Simmer the Jambalaya:** Bring the mixture to a boil, then reduce the heat to low. Cover and simmer for 20-25 minutes, or until the rice is cooked and most of the liquid has been absorbed. Stir occasionally to prevent sticking and ensure even cooking.

4. **Finish and Serve:** Once the rice is tender and the jambalaya has thickened, remove the bay leaves. Adjust seasoning with additional salt, pepper, or cayenne pepper as needed. Serve the vegan jambalaya hot, garnished with chopped fresh parsley and sliced green onions.

Tofu Tikka Masala

🍴 4 servings   🕐 1 hour 10 minutes

INGREDIENTS

For the Tofu Marinade:

- 14 oz (400g) firm tofu, pressed and cut into cubes
- 1/2 cup plain unsweetened plant-based yogurt
- 1 tablespoon lemon juice
- 1 teaspoon ground turmeric
- 1 teaspoon garam masala
- 1 teaspoon ground cumin
- 1/2 teaspoon chili powder
- Salt to taste

For the Tikka Masala Sauce:

- 2 tablespoons olive oil or vegetable oil
- 1 large onion, finely chopped
- 3 cloves garlic, minced
- 1-inch piece of ginger, grated
- 1 can (14 oz) crushed tomatoes
- 1 can (14 oz) coconut milk (full fat for creaminess)
- 1 teaspoon ground turmeric
- 1 teaspoon garam masala
- 1 teaspoon ground coriander
- 1/2 teaspoon chili powder (adjust to taste)
- 1/2 teaspoon ground cumin
- Salt and pepper, to taste
- Fresh cilantro, chopped, for garnish

DIRECTIONS

1. **Marinate the Tofu:** In a bowl, combine the plant-based yogurt, lemon juice, turmeric, garam masala, cumin, chili powder, and salt. Add the tofu cubes and gently toss to coat. Cover and marinate in the refrigerator for at least 30 minutes, or overnight for best results.

2. **Cook the Tofu:** Preheat your oven to 400°F (200°C). Line a baking sheet with parchment paper. Arrange the marinated tofu cubes on the baking sheet in a single layer. Bake for 25-30 minutes, turning halfway through, until the tofu is golden and slightly crispy on the edges.

3. **Prepare the Tikka Masala Sauce:** While the tofu is baking, heat the oil in a large skillet over medium heat. Add the onion, garlic, and ginger. Sauté until the onion is soft and translucent. Add the crushed tomatoes, coconut milk, turmeric, garam masala, coriander, chili powder, cumin, salt, and pepper. Stir to combine. Bring the sauce to a simmer and cook for 10-15 minutes, stirring occasionally, until it thickens slightly.

4. **Combine Tofu and Sauce:** Once the tofu is baked, add it to the skillet with the tikka masala sauce. Gently stir to coat the tofu in the sauce. Continue to simmer for another 5-10 minutes, allowing the tofu to absorb the flavors of the sauce.

5. **Serve:** Garnish the Tofu Tikka Masala with chopped fresh cilantro. Serve hot with steamed rice, naan, or your favorite Indian bread.

Stuffed Bell Peppers with Quinoa and Black Beans

4 servings   75 minutes

INGREDIENTS

- 4 large bell peppers, any color, halved and seeds removed
- 1 cup quinoa, rinsed
- 2 cups vegetable broth
- 1 can (15 oz) black beans, drained and rinsed
- 1 cup corn kernels (fresh, frozen, or canned)
- 1 small onion, diced
- 2 cloves garlic, minced
- 1 teaspoon ground cumin
- 1 teaspoon chili powder
- 1/2 teaspoon smoked paprika
- Salt and pepper, to taste
- 1 cup tomato sauce
- 1/2 cup water
- 1/4 cup fresh cilantro, chopped, plus more for garnish
- Juice of 1 lime
- Optional toppings: avocado slices, vegan cheese, vegan sour cream, lime wedges

DIRECTIONS

1. **Precook the Quinoa:** In a medium saucepan, bring the vegetable broth to a boil. Add the quinoa, reduce heat to low, cover, and simmer for 15-20 minutes, or until all the liquid is absorbed. Remove from heat and let it sit covered for 5 minutes. Fluff with a fork.
2. **Prepare the Filling:** In a large bowl, mix together the cooked quinoa, black beans, corn, onion, garlic, cumin, chili powder, smoked paprika, salt, and pepper. Stir in half of the tomato sauce, the chopped cilantro, and lime juice until well combined.
3. **Stuff the Peppers:** Preheat your oven to 375°F (190°C). Arrange the bell pepper halves in a baking dish, cut-side up. Spoon the quinoa and black bean mixture into each bell pepper half, pressing down slightly to pack the filling.
4. **Bake:** Mix the remaining tomato sauce with 1/2 cup water and pour this around the stuffed peppers in the baking dish. Cover the dish with aluminum foil. Bake in the preheated oven for about 30-40 minutes, or until the peppers are tender and the filling is heated through.
5. **Serve:** Carefully remove the peppers from the oven. Garnish with additional cilantro and any optional toppings like avocado slices, vegan cheese, or a dollop of vegan sour cream. Serve warm with lime wedges on the side.

Vegan Pasta with Broccoli

 4 servings    25 minutes

INGREDIENTS

- 12 oz pasta (choose your favorite shape, whole wheat or gluten-free if preferred)
- 1 large head of broccoli, cut into florets
- 4 tablespoons olive oil, divided
- 4 cloves garlic, minced
- 1/2 teaspoon red pepper flakes (adjust to taste)
- Salt and pepper, to taste
- Juice of 1 lemon
- 1/4 cup nutritional yeast (for a cheesy flavor)
- Fresh parsley, chopped (for garnish)
- Extra lemon wedges, for serving

DIRECTIONS

1. **Cook the Pasta:** Bring a large pot of salted water to a boil. Add the pasta and cook according to the package instructions until al dente. Reserve 1 cup of pasta cooking water before draining.
2. **Blanch the Broccoli:** In the last 3 minutes of the pasta's cooking time, add the broccoli florets to the pot to blanch. Drain the pasta and broccoli together and set aside.
3. **Make the Sauce:** In the same pot, heat 2 tablespoons of olive oil over medium heat. Add the minced garlic and red pepper flakes, sautéing until the garlic is fragrant but not browned, about 1-2 minutes. Add the drained pasta and broccoli back to the pot. Toss well to coat with the garlic oil. If the pasta seems dry, add a little of the reserved pasta water until it reaches your desired consistency.
4. **Season the Pasta:** Stir in the lemon juice, nutritional yeast, and remaining 2 tablespoons of olive oil. Season with salt and pepper to taste. Toss everything together until the pasta and broccoli are well coated with the sauce.
5. **Serve:** Divide the pasta among serving dishes. Garnish with chopped parsley and offer extra lemon wedges on the side.

Vegan Moroccan Tagine

 4-6 servings  55 minutes

INGREDIENTS

- 2 tablespoons olive oil
- 1 large onion, chopped
- 3 cloves garlic, minced
- 2 carrots, peeled and sliced
- 2 sweet potatoes, peeled and cubed
- 1 zucchini, sliced
- 1 bell pepper, any color, chopped
- 1 cup butternut squash, cubed
- 1 can (15 oz) chickpeas, drained and rinsed
- 1 can (14.5 oz) diced tomatoes, undrained
- 1/2 cup dried apricots, chopped
- 1/2 cup raisins or sultanas
- 2 cups vegetable broth
- 1 teaspoon ground cumin
- 1 teaspoon ground cinnamon
- 1/2 teaspoon ground ginger
- 1/2 teaspoon turmeric
- Salt and pepper, to taste
- Fresh cilantro or parsley, chopped (for garnish)
- Cooked couscous or rice, for serving

DIRECTIONS

1. **Sauté the Aromatics:** Heat the olive oil in a large skillet or Dutch oven over medium heat. Add the onion and garlic, sautéing until the onion is translucent, about 5 minutes.
2. **Add Vegetables:** Add the carrots, sweet potatoes, zucchini, bell pepper, and butternut squash to the pot. Stir well to combine and cook for another 5-7 minutes until the vegetables start to soften.
3. **Add Remaining Ingredients:** Stir in the chickpeas, diced tomatoes with their juice, dried apricots, raisins, vegetable broth, cumin, cinnamon, ginger, turmeric, salt, and pepper. Bring the mixture to a simmer.
4. **Simmer the Tagine:** Reduce the heat to low, cover, and simmer for 30-40 minutes, or until the vegetables are tender and the flavors have melded together. Stir occasionally, adding more broth if the stew seems too thick.
5. **Serve:** Taste and adjust the seasoning if necessary. Serve the tagine hot over cooked couscous or rice, garnished with fresh cilantro or parsley.

Creamy Vegan Mushroom Risotto

4 servings   45 minutes

INGREDIENTS

- 1 1/2 cups Arborio rice
- 4 cups vegetable broth, kept warm
- 1 cup white wine (optional, replace with more broth if preferred)
- 2 tablespoons olive oil
- 1 onion, finely chopped
- 2 cloves garlic, minced
- 16 oz mushrooms (such as cremini or button), sliced
- 1 tablespoon fresh thyme leaves or 1 teaspoon dried thyme
- Salt and pepper, to taste
- 1/4 cup nutritional yeast (for a cheesy flavor)
- 2 tablespoons vegan butter
- Fresh parsley, chopped (for garnish)
- Lemon zest, for garnish (optional)

DIRECTIONS

1. **Sauté Onions and Garlic:** In a large, heavy-bottomed saucepan or Dutch oven, heat the olive oil over medium heat. Add the onion and garlic, sautéing until soft and translucent, about 5 minutes.
2. **Cook the Mushrooms:** Add the sliced mushrooms and thyme to the pan. Cook until the mushrooms are golden brown and their liquid has evaporated, about 8-10 minutes. Season with salt and pepper.
3. **Toast the Rice:** Stir in the Arborio rice, toasting it lightly until the edges become translucent, about 2 minutes.
4. **Deglaze with Wine:** Pour in the white wine (if using), scraping any browned bits off the bottom of the pan. Allow the wine to reduce until mostly absorbed.
5. **Add Broth Gradually:** Begin adding the warm vegetable broth, one ladle at a time, stirring frequently. Wait until the broth is almost fully absorbed before adding the next ladle. Continue this process, stirring often, until the rice is creamy and just tender, about 18-20 minutes. If you run out of broth and the rice isn't done, you can add hot water in small amounts until the desired texture is achieved.
6. **Finish the Risotto:** Once the rice is cooked, remove the pan from the heat. Stir in the nutritional yeast and vegan butter until the risotto is creamy and rich. Adjust seasoning with salt and pepper to taste.
7. **Serve:** Serve the risotto hot, garnished with chopped fresh parsley and lemon zest for a bright, fresh finish.

Vegan Lasagna with Cashew Ricotta

 8 servings    70 minutes

INGREDIENTS

For the Cashew Ricotta:

- 2 cups raw cashews, soaked for 4 hours or overnight, then drained
- 1/4 cup nutritional yeast
- 2 tablespoons lemon juice
- 1 clove garlic
- 1/2 cup water (or as needed to blend)
- Salt and pepper, to taste

For the Lasagna:

- 12 lasagna noodles (use gluten-free noodles if necessary)
- 4 cups marinara sauce (store-bought or homemade)
- 2 tablespoons olive oil
- 1 onion, finely chopped
- 3 cloves garlic, minced
- 1 zucchini, sliced
- 1 bell pepper, diced
- 8 oz mushrooms, sliced
- 2 cups spinach or kale, roughly chopped
- 1 teaspoon dried oregano
- 1 teaspoon dried basil
- Salt and pepper, to taste
- Vegan cheese shreds (optional, for topping)

DIRECTIONS

1. **Prepare the Cashew Ricotta:** In a blender or food processor, combine the soaked and drained cashews, nutritional yeast, lemon juice, garlic, and a pinch of salt and pepper. Blend on high, adding water as needed, until the mixture is smooth and resembles the texture of traditional ricotta cheese. Set aside.
2. **Cook the Lasagna Noodles:** Bring a large pot of salted water to a boil. Cook the lasagna noodles according to the package instructions until al dente. Drain and lay the noodles flat on a clean towel to prevent sticking.
3. **Sauté the Vegetables:** In a large skillet, heat the olive oil over medium heat. Add the onion and garlic, sautéing until translucent. Add the zucchini, bell pepper, and mushrooms, cooking until the vegetables are tender. Stir in the spinach or kale until wilted. Season with oregano, basil, salt, and pepper.
4. **Assemble the Lasagna:** Preheat your oven to 375°F (190°C). Spread a thin layer of marinara sauce on the bottom of a 9x13 inch baking dish. Place a layer of lasagna noodles over the sauce. Spread a layer of the cashew ricotta over the noodles, then a layer of the sautéed vegetables. Repeat the layers, finishing with a layer of noodles topped with marinara sauce. Sprinkle vegan cheese shreds on top if using.
5. **Bake:** Cover the baking dish with aluminum foil and bake for 25 minutes. Remove the foil and bake for an additional 15 minutes, or until the top is bubbly and slightly golden.
6. **Serve:** Let the lasagna cool for 10-15 minutes before slicing and serving. Garnish with fresh basil or parsley if desired.

Vegan Thai Curry with Vegetables

🍴 4-6 servings 🕐 40 minutes

INGREDIENTS

- 2 tablespoons coconut oil
- 1 onion, sliced
- 2 cloves garlic, minced
- 1 tablespoon fresh ginger, grated
- 2–3 tablespoons Thai red curry paste (adjust according to taste and brand)
- 1 can (14 oz) coconut milk
- 1 cup vegetable broth
- 1 tablespoon soy sauce or tamari (for a gluten-free option)
- 1 tablespoon maple syrup or sugar
- 1 red bell pepper, sliced
- 1 yellow bell pepper, sliced
- 1 zucchini, sliced
- 1 carrot, julienned
- 1 cup broccoli florets
- 1 block (14 oz) firm tofu, pressed and cubed
- Salt, to taste
- Juice of 1 lime
- Fresh basil or cilantro, for garnish
- Cooked jasmine or basmati rice, for serving

DIRECTIONS

1. **Sauté Aromatics:** Heat the coconut oil in a large skillet or wok over medium heat. Add the onion, garlic, and ginger, and sauté until the onion is translucent and fragrant, about 5 minutes.
2. **Add Curry Paste:** Stir in the Thai red curry paste and cook for 1–2 minutes until fragrant.
3. **Simmer with Coconut Milk:** Pour in the coconut milk, vegetable broth, soy sauce, and maple syrup. Stir well to combine the curry paste with the liquids. Bring the mixture to a simmer.
4. **Add Vegetables and Tofu:** Add the red and yellow bell peppers, zucchini, carrot, and broccoli to the skillet. Stir well to coat the vegetables in the curry sauce. Gently fold in the cubed tofu, being careful not to break it. Season with salt, to taste. Let the curry simmer for 10-15 minutes, or until the vegetables are tender but still crisp.
5. **Finish and Serve:** Stir in the lime juice just before serving. Taste and adjust seasoning if necessary. Serve the curry hot, garnished with fresh basil or cilantro, over cooked rice.

Vegan Gnocchi with Tomato Basil Sauce

🍴 4 servings   🕐 30 minutes

INGREDIENTS

- 1 (16 oz) package vegan gnocchi
- 2 tablespoons olive oil
- 1 onion, finely chopped
- 3 cloves garlic, minced
- 1 can (28 oz) crushed tomatoes
- Salt and pepper, to taste
- 1 teaspoon sugar (optional, to balance acidity)
- 1/2 cup fresh basil, chopped, plus more for garnish
- Vegan Parmesan cheese (optional, for serving)

DIRECTIONS

1. **Cook the Gnocchi:** Bring a large pot of salted water to a boil. Add the gnocchi and cook according to the package instructions, usually 2-3 minutes or until they float to the surface. Drain and set aside.
2. **Prepare the Tomato Basil Sauce:** While the gnocchi is cooking, heat the olive oil in a large skillet over medium heat. Add the onion and garlic, sautéing until soft and translucent, about 5 minutes. Stir in the crushed tomatoes, salt, pepper, and sugar (if using). Simmer the sauce for about 10-15 minutes, allowing the flavors to meld together. Just before serving, stir in the chopped fresh basil.
3. **Combine Gnocchi and Sauce:** Add the cooked gnocchi to the skillet with the tomato basil sauce. Gently toss to coat the gnocchi evenly with the sauce.
4. **Serve:** Divide the gnocchi among serving plates. Garnish with additional fresh basil and sprinkle with vegan Parmesan cheese if desired.

Vegan Fajitas with Portobello Mushrooms

☆☆☆☆☆

 4 servings  40 minutes

INGREDIENTS

- 3 large portobello mushrooms, sliced
- 1 red bell pepper, sliced
- 1 yellow bell pepper, sliced
- 1 green bell pepper, sliced
- 1 large onion, sliced
- 2 tablespoons olive oil
- 1 teaspoon ground cumin
- 1 teaspoon smoked paprika
- 1/2 teaspoon chili powder
- 1/2 teaspoon garlic powder
- Salt and pepper, to taste
- Juice of 1 lime
- Warm tortillas, for serving
- Optional toppings: sliced avocado, fresh cilantro, lime wedges, vegan sour cream, and salsa

DIRECTIONS

1. **Preheat the Oven (or Grill):** Preheat your oven to 425°F (220°C) if baking. Alternatively, you can cook the fajitas on a grill or stovetop grill pan for a more charred flavor.

2. **Season the Vegetables:** In a large bowl, combine the sliced portobello mushrooms, bell peppers, and onion. Drizzle with olive oil, then add cumin, smoked paprika, chili powder, garlic powder, salt, and pepper. Toss until the vegetables are evenly coated with the oil and seasonings.

3. **Cook the Fajitas:**
   - **Oven Method:** Spread the vegetables on a large baking sheet in a single layer. Roast in the preheated oven for 20-25 minutes, or until the vegetables are tender and slightly charred at the edges. Stir halfway through cooking.
   - **Grill Method:** Preheat the grill or grill pan to medium-high heat. Cook the vegetables in a grill basket or directly on the grill, stirring occasionally, for about 10-15 minutes, or until tender and charred to your liking.

4. **Finish and Serve:** Squeeze lime juice over the cooked vegetables and give them a final toss. Serve the vegetable mixture hot, with warm tortillas and your choice of toppings like sliced avocado, fresh cilantro, lime wedges, vegan sour cream, and salsa.

Vegan Bolognese with Lentils

🍴 4-6 servings   🕐 80 minutes

INGREDIENTS

- 1 cup dried green or brown lentils, rinsed
- 2 tablespoons olive oil
- 1 large onion, finely chopped
- 2 carrots, diced
- 2 celery stalks, diced
- 3 cloves garlic, minced
- 1 can (28 oz) crushed tomatoes
- 2 tablespoons tomato paste
- 1 cup vegetable broth
- 1 teaspoon dried oregano
- 1 teaspoon dried basil
- 1/2 teaspoon dried thyme
- 1 bay leaf
- Salt and pepper, to taste
- 1/2 cup red wine (optional, can replace with more broth)
- 2 tablespoons nutritional yeast (for a cheesy flavor)
- Fresh basil, chopped, for garnish
- Cooked pasta of your choice, for serving

DIRECTIONS

1. **Cook the Lentils:** In a medium saucepan, combine the lentils with enough water to cover by a couple of inches. Bring to a boil, then reduce heat and simmer for 20-25 minutes, or until the lentils are tender but not mushy. Drain and set aside.
2. **Sauté the Vegetables:** Heat the olive oil in a large skillet or saucepan over medium heat. Add the onion, carrots, celery, and garlic. Sauté until the vegetables are softened, about 5-7 minutes.
3. **Add Tomatoes and Lentils:** Stir in the crushed tomatoes, tomato paste, cooked lentils, vegetable broth, oregano, basil, thyme, and bay leaf. If using, add the red wine. Season with salt and pepper.
4. **Simmer the Bolognese:** Bring the mixture to a simmer, then reduce heat to low. Cover and let it cook for 30-40 minutes, stirring occasionally. If the sauce becomes too thick, add a little more broth to reach your desired consistency.
5. **Finish the Sauce:** Remove the bay leaf and stir in the nutritional yeast. Adjust the seasoning if needed.
6. **Serve:** Serve the vegan Bolognese sauce over cooked pasta, garnished with fresh basil.

Vegan Ramen with Miso Broth

 4 servings    40 minutes

INGREDIENTS

For the Miso Broth:

- 4 cups vegetable broth
- 2 cups water
- 3 tablespoons miso paste (white or red, or a mix)
- 1 tablespoon soy sauce or tamari (for gluten-free)
- 1 tablespoon sesame oil
- 2 cloves garlic, minced
- 1 inch piece ginger, grated
- 1 tablespoon rice vinegar

For the Ramen Bowl:

- 4 servings ramen noodles (use vegan noodles, and check for gluten-free if necessary)
- 1 block (14 oz) firm tofu, pressed and cubed
- 2 tablespoons olive oil, divided
- Salt and pepper, to taste
- 1 cup mushrooms, sliced (shiitake, cremini, or button)
- 1 cup spinach or baby bok choy
- 1 carrot, julienned
- 2 green onions, sliced
- 1 sheet nori, cut into strips
- Sesame seeds, for garnish

DIRECTIONS

1. **Prepare the Miso Broth:** In a large pot, combine the vegetable broth and water and bring to a simmer over medium heat. In a small bowl, mix the miso paste with a little hot broth until smooth. Stir the miso mixture, soy sauce, sesame oil, garlic, ginger, and rice vinegar into the pot. Reduce the heat to low, ensuring the broth doesn't boil to preserve the miso's probiotics.

2. **Cook the Tofu:** Heat 1 tablespoon of olive oil in a skillet over medium-high heat. Season the tofu cubes with salt and pepper, and fry until all sides are golden brown. Set aside.

3. **Cook the Vegetables:** In the same skillet, add another tablespoon of olive oil and sauté the mushrooms until tender. Remove and set aside. Quickly blanch the spinach or bok choy and carrot in boiling water for 1-2 minutes. Drain and set aside.

4. **Cook the Ramen Noodles:** Cook the ramen noodles according to the package instructions, drain well, and divide among serving bowls.

5. **Assemble the Ramen Bowls:** Ladle the hot miso broth over the noodles in each bowl. Arrange the cooked tofu, sautéed mushrooms, spinach or bok choy, julienned carrot, and sliced green onions on top of the noodles.

6. **Serve:** Garnish each bowl with nori strips and sesame seeds. Serve immediately, allowing each person to stir their bowl to mix the ingredients with the broth.

Vegan Enchiladas with Black Beans

☆☆☆☆☆

🍴 4-6 servings   🕐 55 minutes

INGREDIENTS

For the Enchiladas:

- 2 cups black beans, cooked and drained (or 1 can of black beans, rinsed and drained)
- 1 onion, finely chopped
- 2 cloves garlic, minced
- 1 bell pepper, diced
- 1 zucchini, diced
- 1 cup corn kernels (fresh, frozen, or canned)
- 2 teaspoons cumin
- 1 teaspoon smoked paprika
- Salt and pepper, to taste
- 8-10 flour tortillas (use gluten-free if necessary)
- 2 cups vegan cheese shreds (optional)
- Fresh cilantro, for garnish

For the Enchilada Sauce:

- 2 tablespoons olive oil
- 2 tablespoons all-purpose flour (use gluten-free if needed)
- 1 tablespoon chili powder
- 1 teaspoon cumin
- 2 cups vegetable broth
- 1 can (8 oz) tomato sauce
- Salt and pepper, to taste

DIRECTIONS

1. **Make the Enchilada Sauce:** In a saucepan over medium heat, heat the olive oil. Whisk in the flour, chili powder, and cumin, cooking for 1 minute until fragrant. Gradually add the vegetable broth, whisking continuously to prevent lumps. Stir in the tomato sauce. Bring to a simmer and cook until slightly thickened, about 5-7 minutes. Season with salt and pepper. Set aside.

2. **Prepare the Filling:** In a large skillet over medium heat, sauté the onion and garlic until soft. Add the bell pepper, zucchini, and corn, cooking until just tender. Stir in the black beans, cumin, smoked paprika, salt, and pepper. Cook for an additional 2-3 minutes. Remove from heat.

3. **Assemble the Enchiladas:** Preheat your oven to 375°F (190°C). Spread a thin layer of enchilada sauce on the bottom of a baking dish. Fill each tortilla with the bean and vegetable mixture (and vegan cheese if using), roll tightly, and place seam-side down in the baking dish. Repeat with the remaining tortillas. Pour the remaining enchilada sauce over the rolled enchiladas, covering them thoroughly. Sprinkle with vegan cheese shreds if desired.

4. **Bake:** Cover the baking dish with aluminum foil and bake for 20 minutes. Remove the foil and bake for an additional 10 minutes, or until the enchiladas are heated through and the top is slightly golden.

5. **Serve:** Let the enchiladas cool slightly before serving. Garnish with fresh cilantro and serve hot.

Vegan Moussaka with Eggplant and Lentils

 4-6 servings  55 minutes

INGREDIENTS

For the Eggplant:

- 2 large eggplants, sliced into 1/4 inch rounds
- Olive oil, for brushing
- Salt and pepper, to taste

For the Lentil Tomato Sauce:

- 1 cup dried green lentils, rinsed
- 2 tablespoons olive oil
- 1 onion, finely chopped
- 2 cloves garlic, minced
- 1 can (14 oz) crushed tomatoes
- 2 tablespoons tomato paste
- 1 teaspoon dried oregano
- 1 teaspoon smoked paprika
- Salt and pepper, to taste
- 1/2 cup red wine (optional)

For the Vegan Béchamel:

- 1/4 cup olive oil
- 1/4 cup all-purpose flour (use gluten-free if needed)
- 2 cups unsweetened almond milk (or any plant-based milk)
- Nutmeg, a pinch
- Salt and pepper, to taste
- 1/4 cup nutritional yeast, for a cheesy flavor

DIRECTIONS

1. **Roast the Eggplant:** Preheat your oven to 400°F (200°C). Line two baking sheets with parchment paper. Arrange the eggplant slices in a single layer on the sheets. Brush both sides with olive oil and season with salt and pepper. Roast for 20-25 minutes, flipping halfway through, until golden and soft. Set aside.

2. **Prepare the Lentil Tomato Sauce:** While the eggplant is roasting, cook the lentils in boiling water for 20-25 minutes until tender but not mushy. Drain and set aside. In a large skillet, heat the olive oil over medium heat. Sauté the onion and garlic until soft. Stir in the crushed tomatoes, tomato paste, oregano, smoked paprika, salt, pepper, and red wine if using. Add the cooked lentils and simmer for 10 minutes, allowing the flavors to meld. Adjust seasoning as needed.

3. **Make the Vegan Béchamel:** In a saucepan, heat the olive oil over medium heat. Whisk in the flour to form a roux. Gradually add the almond milk, whisking constantly to prevent lumps. Cook until the sauce thickens. Season with nutmeg, salt, pepper, and stir in the nutritional yeast. Remove from heat.

4. **Assemble the Moussaka:** In a greased baking dish, layer half of the roasted eggplant slices. Spread half of the lentil tomato sauce over the eggplant. Repeat with another layer of eggplant and lentil sauce. Pour the béchamel sauce over the top, spreading it evenly.

5. **Bake:** Bake in the preheated oven for 35-40 minutes, or until the top is golden and the sauce is bubbly.

6. **Serve:** Allow the moussaka to cool for 10-15 minutes before slicing. Serve warm, garnished with chopped parsley or fresh herbs if desired.

Creamy Vegan Carbonara with Smoked Almonds

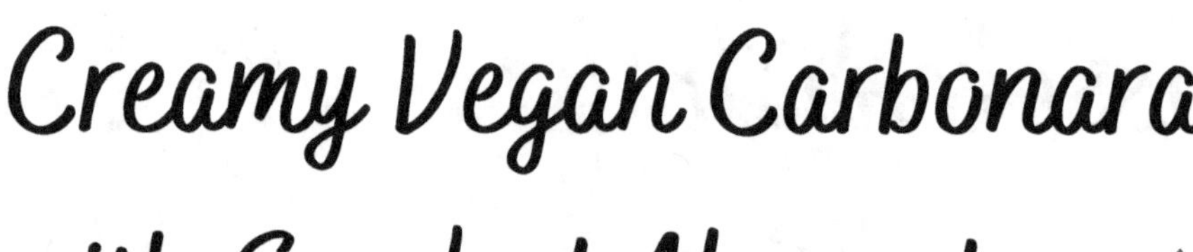

☆☆☆☆☆

🍴 4 servings   🕐 35 minutes

INGREDIENTS

For the Pasta:

- 12 oz spaghetti or fettuccine (use gluten-free pasta if necessary)

For the Creamy Sauce:

- 1 cup raw cashews, soaked for 4 hours or overnight, then drained
- 1 cup unsweetened almond milk (or any plant-based milk)
- 2 tablespoons nutritional yeast
- 1 tablespoon lemon juice
- 2 cloves garlic
- Salt and pepper, to taste

For the Smoked Almonds:

- 1/2 cup almonds, roughly chopped
- 1/2 teaspoon smoked paprika
- 1 tablespoon olive oil
- Salt, to taste

Additional Ingredients:

- 2 tablespoons olive oil
- 1 onion, finely chopped
- 8 oz mushrooms, sliced
- 1/2 cup frozen peas, thawed
- Fresh parsley, chopped, for garnish

DIRECTIONS

1. **Prepare the Pasta:** Cook the pasta according to the package instructions in a large pot of salted boiling water until al dente. Drain, reserving 1 cup of pasta water, and set aside.
2. **Make the Creamy Sauce:** In a blender, combine the soaked and drained cashews, almond milk, nutritional yeast, lemon juice, garlic, salt, and pepper. Blend until smooth and creamy. If the sauce is too thick, add a bit of the reserved pasta water to reach your desired consistency.
3. **Prepare the Smoked Almonds:** In a small bowl, toss the chopped almonds with smoked paprika, olive oil, and salt. Spread them on a baking sheet and bake in a preheated oven at 350°F (175°C) for 5-7 minutes, or until golden and fragrant. Set aside to cool.
4. **Sauté the Vegetables:** In a large skillet, heat 2 tablespoons of olive oil over medium heat. Add the onion and mushrooms, sautéing until the mushrooms are golden and the onions are translucent. Stir in the thawed peas and cook for an additional 2 minutes.
5. **Combine and Serve:** Add the cooked pasta to the skillet with the vegetables. Pour the creamy sauce over the pasta, tossing to coat evenly. If the sauce is too thick, add a bit more of the reserved pasta water. Serve the pasta hot, sprinkled with the smoked almonds and garnished with fresh parsley.

Desserts

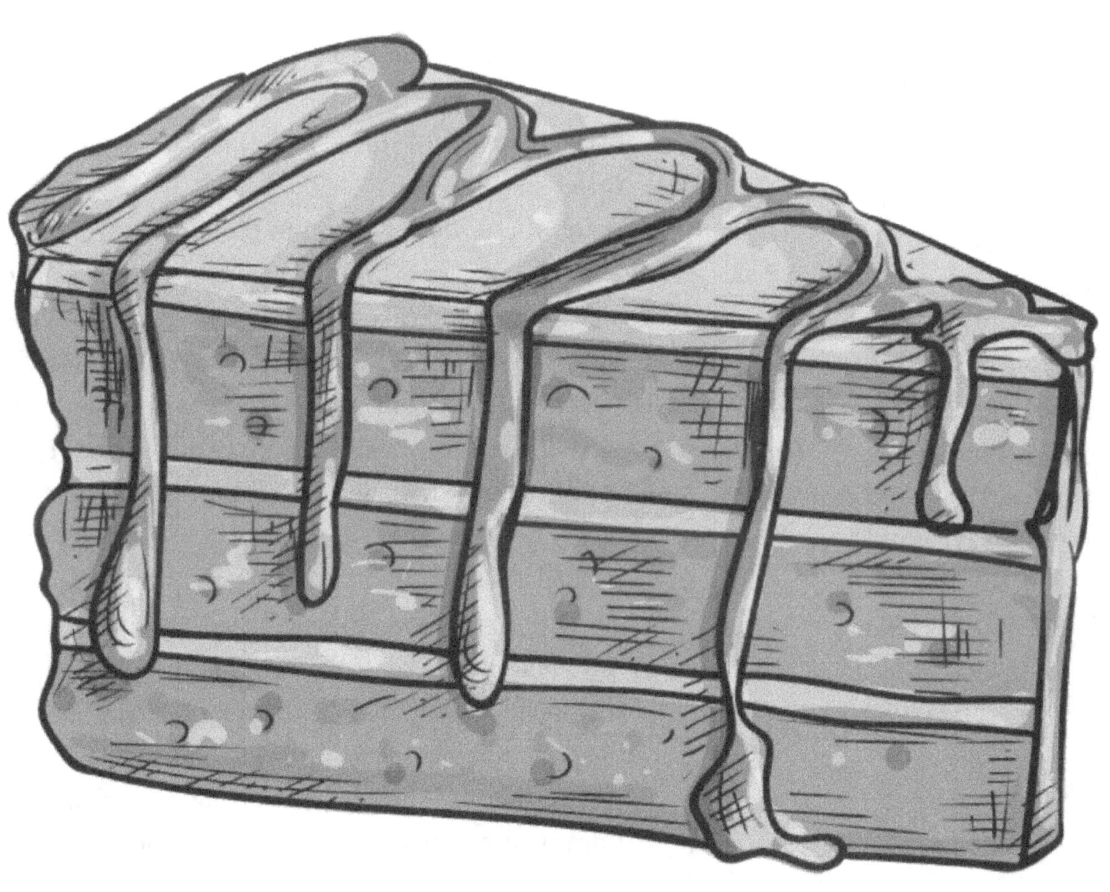

Vegan Chocolate Cake

🍴 8-10 servings　🕐 1 hour

INGREDIENTS

For the Cake:
- 1 1/2 cups all-purpose flour
- 1 cup granulated sugar
- 1/2 cup cocoa powder
- 1 teaspoon baking soda
- 1/2 teaspoon salt
- 1 cup unsweetened plant-based milk (such as almond, soy, or oat milk)
- 1/3 cup vegetable oil
- 2 tablespoons apple cider vinegar
- 1 teaspoon vanilla extract

For the Vegan Chocolate Frosting:
- 1/2 cup vegan butter, softened
- 2 cups powdered sugar, sifted
- 3/4 cup cocoa powder, sifted
- 1/4 cup unsweetened plant-based milk, as needed
- 1 teaspoon vanilla extract

DIRECTIONS

1. **Preheat the Oven and Prepare the Pans:** Preheat your oven to 350°F (175°C). Grease two 8-inch round cake pans and line the bottoms with parchment paper for easy removal.

2. **Make the Cake Batter:** In a large mixing bowl, whisk together the flour, sugar, cocoa powder, baking soda, and salt. Add the plant-based milk, vegetable oil, apple cider vinegar, and vanilla extract. Mix until just combined; avoid overmixing. Divide the batter evenly between the prepared cake pans.

3. **Bake the Cake:** Bake for 25-30 minutes, or until a toothpick inserted into the center of the cakes comes out clean. Allow the cakes to cool in the pans for 10 minutes, then transfer them to a wire rack to cool completely.

4. **Prepare the Vegan Chocolate Frosting:** In a medium mixing bowl, use an electric mixer to beat the vegan butter until creamy. Gradually add the powdered sugar and cocoa powder, alternating with splashes of plant-based milk as needed, until the frosting reaches your desired consistency and sweetness. Mix in the vanilla extract.

5. **Assemble the Cake:** If the cakes have domed on top, trim them with a knife to make them level. Place one cake layer on your serving plate and spread a generous layer of frosting on top. Place the second cake layer on top and use the remaining frosting to cover the top and sides of the cake.

6. **Serve:** Let the cake set for a few minutes before slicing. Serve and enjoy!

Coconut Milk Ice Cream

4 hours
30 minutes

INGREDIENTS

Basic Coconut Milk Ice Cream:

- 2 cans (13.5 oz each) full-fat coconut milk
- 2/3 cup granulated sugar or maple syrup (adjust sweetness to taste)
- 1 teaspoon vanilla extract

Optional Flavor Add-Ins:

- For Chocolate: 1/2 cup cocoa powder or melted vegan chocolate
- For Strawberry: 1 cup fresh strawberries, pureed
- For Mint Chocolate Chip: 1 teaspoon peppermint extract and 1/2 cup vegan chocolate chips

DIRECTIONS

1. **Chill the Coconut Milk:** For the creamiest ice cream, refrigerate the cans of coconut milk overnight. This allows the cream to separate and solidify, making your ice cream richer.
2. **Prepare the Ice Cream Base:** Scoop the solidified coconut cream into a blender, leaving behind any coconut water at the bottom of the can (use it in smoothies or cooking). Add the sugar or maple syrup and vanilla extract to the blender. Blend on high until the mixture is completely smooth.
3. **Add Flavorings (Optional):** If you're making a flavored ice cream, add your chosen flavor add-ins to the blender and mix until well combined.
4. **Churn the Ice Cream:** Pour the mixture into an ice cream maker and churn according to the manufacturer's instructions, usually about 20-25 minutes, until it reaches a soft-serve consistency. If you're adding mix-ins like chocolate chips or fruit pieces, fold them in after churning.
5. **Freeze:** Transfer the churned ice cream to a freezer-safe container. Cover the surface with parchment paper to prevent ice crystals from forming. Freeze for at least 4 hours, or until firm.
6. **Serve:** Remove the ice cream from the freezer about 10 minutes before serving to soften slightly for easier scooping. Serve in bowls or cones, and enjoy!

Banana Bread (Vegan)

🕐 1 hour 15 minutes

INGREDIENTS

- 1 3/4 cups all-purpose flour (or substitute with whole wheat flour for a healthier option)
- 1/2 cup granulated sugar
- 1/2 cup brown sugar, packed
- 1/2 teaspoon salt
- 1 teaspoon baking soda
- 1/2 teaspoon ground cinnamon (optional)
- 1/3 cup vegetable oil or melted coconut oil
- 4 ripe bananas, mashed (about 2 cups)
- 1/4 cup plant-based milk (such as almond, soy, or oat milk)
- 1 teaspoon apple cider vinegar
- 1 teaspoon vanilla extract
- 1/2 cup walnuts or pecans, chopped (optional)
- 1/2 cup vegan chocolate chips (optional)

DIRECTIONS

1. **Preheat the Oven and Prepare the Pan:** Preheat your oven to 350°F (175°C). Grease a 9x5-inch loaf pan or line it with parchment paper for easy removal.
2. **Mix Dry Ingredients:** In a large bowl, whisk together the flour, granulated sugar, brown sugar, salt, baking soda, and cinnamon (if using).
3. **Combine Wet Ingredients:** In another bowl, mix the vegetable oil, mashed bananas, plant-based milk, apple cider vinegar, and vanilla extract until well combined.
4. **Combine Wet and Dry Ingredients:** Add the wet ingredients to the dry ingredients, stirring until just combined. Be careful not to overmix. If using, fold in the chopped nuts and/or vegan chocolate chips.
5. **Bake:** Pour the batter into the prepared loaf pan and smooth the top with a spatula. Bake in the preheated oven for 55-65 minutes, or until a toothpick inserted into the center of the bread comes out clean.
6. **Cool:** Let the banana bread cool in the pan for about 10 minutes, then transfer it to a wire rack to cool completely.
7. **Serve:** Slice and serve the banana bread once it's cooled. Enjoy as is, or spread with vegan butter or cream cheese for extra indulgence.

Raspberry Sorbet

 4 hours

INGREDIENTS

- 4 cups fresh raspberries (you can also use frozen raspberries, thawed)
- 3/4 cup granulated sugar (adjust according to taste and the sweetness of the raspberries)
- 1 cup water
- Juice of 1 lemon

DIRECTIONS

1. **Make the Simple Syrup:** In a small saucepan, combine the water and sugar. Heat over medium heat, stirring occasionally, until the sugar has completely dissolved. Allow the simple syrup to cool to room temperature, then chill in the refrigerator until cold.
2. **Puree the Raspberries:** Place the raspberries in a blender or food processor. Add the lemon juice and blend until smooth. If desired, you can strain the puree through a fine-mesh sieve to remove the seeds, but this step is optional.
3. **Combine and Chill:** Mix the raspberry puree with the chilled simple syrup. Stir well to combine. Cover and chill the mixture in the refrigerator for at least 1-2 hours, or until completely cold.
4. **Churn the Sorbet:** Pour the chilled raspberry mixture into an ice cream maker and churn according to the manufacturer's instructions, usually about 20-30 minutes, until it reaches a soft-serve consistency.
5. **Freeze:** Transfer the sorbet to a freezer-safe container. Cover and freeze until firm, about 2-4 hours.
6. **Serve:** Before serving, let the sorbet sit at room temperature for a few minutes to soften slightly for easier scooping. Serve in bowls or cones, garnished with fresh raspberries or mint leaves if desired.

Vegan Cheesecake

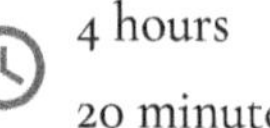

8-10 servings   4 hours 20 minutes

INGREDIENTS

For the Crust:

- 1 1/2 cups graham cracker crumbs (use vegan graham crackers)
- 1/4 cup coconut oil, melted
- 2 tablespoons sugar (optional)

For the Filling:

- 2 cups raw cashews, soaked overnight and drained
- 1 can (13.5 oz) full-fat coconut cream, chilled
- 1/2 cup maple syrup or agave syrup
- 1/4 cup lemon juice
- 2 teaspoons vanilla extract
- Zest of 1 lemon (optional for extra flavor)
- Pinch of salt

DIRECTIONS

1. **Prepare the Crust:** Preheat your oven to 350°F (175°C). Grease a 9-inch springform pan with a little coconut oil or line it with parchment paper. In a mixing bowl, combine the graham cracker crumbs, melted coconut oil, and sugar (if using) until well mixed. Press the mixture firmly into the bottom of the prepared pan. Bake the crust for 10 minutes, then remove from the oven and let it cool while you prepare the filling.
2. **Make the Filling:** In a high-speed blender or food processor, combine the soaked and drained cashews, coconut cream (scoop out the cream and leave the liquid behind), maple syrup, lemon juice, vanilla extract, lemon zest (if using), and a pinch of salt. Blend until the mixture is completely smooth and creamy. This may take a few minutes, and you might need to scrape down the sides a few times.
3. **Assemble the Cheesecake:** Pour the filling over the cooled crust and smooth the top with a spatula. Tap the pan gently on the counter to remove any air bubbles.
4. **Chill the Cheesecake:** Cover the cheesecake and refrigerate for at least 4 hours, or overnight, until it is firm and set.
5. **Serve:** Once set, carefully remove the cheesecake from the springform pan. If desired, top with fresh berries, fruit compote, or vegan whipped cream before serving.

Churros with Chocolate Sauce

☆☆☆☆☆

🍴 20-24 churros   🕐 30 minutes

INGREDIENTS

For the Churros:
- 1 cup water
- 2 1/2 tablespoons granulated sugar
- 1/2 teaspoon salt
- 2 tablespoons vegetable oil
- 1 cup all-purpose flour
- Vegetable oil for frying

For the Sugar Coating:
- 1/2 cup granulated sugar
- 1 teaspoon ground cinnamon

For the Chocolate Sauce:
- 1 cup heavy cream or full-fat coconut milk (for a vegan option)
- 1 cup chopped dark chocolate or chocolate chips (ensure vegan if needed)
- Optional: A pinch of ground cinnamon or chili powder for extra flavor

DIRECTIONS

1. **Make the Churro Dough:** In a medium saucepan, combine water, 2 1/2 tablespoons sugar, salt, and 2 tablespoons oil. Bring to a boil over medium heat. Reduce the heat to low and stir in the flour until the mixture forms a ball. Remove from heat and let the dough cool slightly.
2. **Prepare the Sugar Coating:** Mix 1/2 cup sugar and 1 teaspoon cinnamon in a shallow dish. Set aside.
3. **Heat the Oil for Frying:** In a deep skillet or saucepan, heat about 2 inches of vegetable oil to 375°F (190°C).
4. **Pipe and Fry the Churros:** Spoon the churro dough into a piping bag fitted with a large star tip. Pipe strips of dough into the hot oil, cutting them with scissors at your desired length. Fry the churros, turning them occasionally, until they are golden brown on all sides, about 2-3 minutes. Using a slotted spoon, transfer the churros to a paper towel-lined plate to drain.
5. **Coat the Churros:** While the churros are still warm, roll them in the cinnamon-sugar mixture until well coated.
6. **Make the Chocolate Sauce:** Heat the heavy cream or coconut milk in a small saucepan over medium heat until it begins to simmer. Remove from heat and add the chopped chocolate or chocolate chips. Let sit for 1 minute, then stir until smooth and glossy. Add a pinch of cinnamon or chili powder if desired.
7. **Serve:** Serve the warm churros with the chocolate sauce for dipping.

Vegan Apple Pie

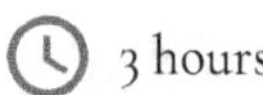
3 hours

INGREDIENTS

For the Pie Crust:
- 2 1/2 cups all-purpose flour
- 1 teaspoon salt
- 1 tablespoon sugar (optional)
- 1 cup vegan butter, cold and cut into small pieces
- 4-8 tablespoons ice water

For the Apple Filling:
- 5-6 large apples (a mix of Granny Smith and your favorite sweet variety), peeled, cored, and thinly sliced
- 3/4 cup granulated sugar
- 2 tablespoons all-purpose flour
- 2 tablespoons cornstarch
- 1 teaspoon ground cinnamon
- 1/4 teaspoon ground nutmeg
- 1/4 teaspoon salt
- Juice of 1/2 lemon
- 1 teaspoon vanilla extract

For Assembly:
- 1 tablespoon plant-based milk (for brushing the crust)
- 1 tablespoon coarse sugar, for sprinkling on top (optional)

DIRECTIONS

1. **Prepare the Pie Crust:** In a large bowl, combine flour, salt, and sugar (if using). Add the cold vegan butter and use a pastry cutter or fork to blend the butter into the flour until the mixture resembles coarse crumbs. Gradually add ice water, 1 tablespoon at a time, mixing just until the dough comes together. Divide the dough in half, form into discs, wrap in plastic wrap, and refrigerate for at least 1 hour.

2. **Make the Apple Filling:** In a large bowl, toss the sliced apples with sugar, flour, cornstarch, cinnamon, nutmeg, salt, lemon juice, and vanilla extract. Let sit for about 15 minutes to allow the flavors to meld and the apples to release their juices.

3. **Assemble the Pie:** Preheat your oven to 425°F (220°C). On a floured surface, roll out one disc of dough into a circle large enough to fit your pie dish. Transfer it to the dish, gently pressing into the bottom and sides. Fill the crust with the apple mixture, mounding slightly in the center. Roll out the second disc of dough and place it over the filling. Trim any excess dough and crimp the edges to seal. Cut a few slits in the top crust to allow steam to escape. Brush the top crust with plant-based milk and sprinkle with coarse sugar, if desired.

4. **Bake:** Place the pie on a baking sheet to catch any drips. Bake for 20 minutes at 425°F (220°C), then reduce the temperature to 350°F (175°C) and continue baking for another 30-35 minutes, or until the crust is golden and the filling is bubbly. If the edges of the crust start to brown too quickly, cover them with foil.

5. **Cool and Serve:** Let the pie cool on a wire rack for at least 2 hours before serving. This allows the filling to set.

Avocado Chocolate Mousse

2-4 servings · 30-60 minutes

INGREDIENTS

- 2 ripe avocados, peeled and pitted
- 1/2 cup cocoa powder (unsweetened)
- 1/4 cup maple syrup or agave nectar (adjust to taste)
- 1 teaspoon vanilla extract
- Pinch of salt
- Optional toppings: fresh berries, chopped nuts, shredded coconut, or whipped coconut cream

DIRECTIONS

1. **Blend the Avocados:** In a food processor or blender, combine the ripe avocados, cocoa powder, maple syrup or agave nectar, vanilla extract, and a pinch of salt.
2. **Blend Until Smooth:** Blend the ingredients until the mixture is smooth and creamy. You may need to stop and scrape down the sides of the blender or food processor a few times to ensure everything is well combined.
3. **Taste and Adjust:** Taste the chocolate mousse and adjust the sweetness or cocoa flavor to your liking. Add more maple syrup for sweetness or more cocoa powder for a richer chocolate flavor.
4. **Chill (Optional):** For a firmer texture, you can chill the chocolate mousse in the refrigerator for 30 minutes to 1 hour before serving. This also allows the flavors to meld together.
5. **Serve:** Divide the chocolate mousse into serving dishes or glasses. Garnish with your favorite toppings, such as fresh berries, chopped nuts, shredded coconut, or a dollop of whipped coconut cream.
6. **Enjoy:** Serve the avocado chocolate mousse immediately and enjoy its creamy, chocolatey goodness!

Vegan Raspberry and Pistachio Cheesecake

 8-10 servings 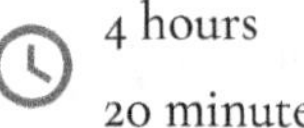 4 hours 20 minutes

INGREDIENTS

For the Crust:

- 1 cup pistachios, shelled
- 1 cup medjool dates, pitted
- 1/2 cup rolled oats (use gluten-free if needed)
- A pinch of salt

For the Filling:

- 2 cups raw cashews, soaked for 4 hours or overnight, then drained
- 1 cup raspberries (fresh or thawed if frozen)
- 1/2 cup coconut cream
- 1/2 cup maple syrup or agave nectar
- 1/4 cup coconut oil, melted
- Juice of 1 lemon
- 1 teaspoon vanilla extract

For the Topping:

- 1/2 cup raspberries
- 1/4 cup pistachios, shelled and chopped
- Optional: Mint leaves, for garnish

DIRECTIONS

1. **Prepare the Crust:** In a food processor, combine pistachios, dates, rolled oats, and a pinch of salt. Process until the mixture sticks together when pinched. Press the mixture firmly into the bottom of a greased or parchment-lined 8-inch springform pan. Set in the freezer to firm up while you prepare the filling.
2. **Make the Filling:** In a high-speed blender, blend the soaked and drained cashews, raspberries, coconut cream, maple syrup, melted coconut oil, lemon juice, and vanilla extract until smooth and creamy. Pour the filling over the prepared crust and smooth the top with a spatula.
3. **Chill the Cheesecake:** Place the cheesecake in the freezer for at least 4 hours, or until set.
4. **Prepare the Topping:** Just before serving, top the cheesecake with fresh raspberries and chopped pistachios. Garnish with mint leaves if desired.
5. **Serve:** Allow the cheesecake to sit at room temperature for 10-15 minutes before slicing and serving. This will make it easier to cut and improve the texture for eating.

Vegan Tiramisu

8-10 servings   5 hours

INGREDIENTS

For the Sponge Layers:

- 1 cup all-purpose flour (use gluten-free if needed)
- 1/2 cup almond flour
- 3/4 cup granulated sugar
- 1 teaspoon baking powder
- 1/2 teaspoon baking soda
- 1 cup almond milk
- 1/3 cup vegetable oil
- 1 teaspoon apple cider vinegar
- 1 teaspoon vanilla extract

For the Coffee Soak:

- 1 cup strong brewed coffee, cooled
- 2 tablespoons coffee liqueur (optional)

For the Cream Filling:

- 1 1/2 cups raw cashews, soaked for 4 hours or overnight and drained
- 1/2 cup canned coconut cream
- 1/2 cup powdered sugar
- 2 tablespoons lemon juice
- 1 teaspoon vanilla extract

For Assembly:

- Cocoa powder, for dusting
- Vegan chocolate shavings (optional)

DIRECTIONS

1. **Prepare the Sponge:** Preheat your oven to 350°F (175°C). Line a 9x9 inch baking pan with parchment paper. In a large bowl, whisk together all-purpose flour, almond flour, granulated sugar, baking powder, and baking soda. In another bowl, mix almond milk, vegetable oil, apple cider vinegar, and vanilla extract. Add the wet ingredients to the dry ingredients and mix until smooth. Pour the batter into the prepared pan and bake for 25-30 minutes, or until a toothpick inserted into the center comes out clean. Allow to cool completely.

2. **Prepare the Coffee Soak:** In a shallow dish, combine the cooled coffee and coffee liqueur if using. Set aside.

3. **Make the Cream Filling:** In a blender, combine the soaked and drained cashews, coconut cream, powdered sugar, lemon juice, and vanilla extract. Blend until smooth and creamy.

4. **Assemble the Tiramisu:** Slice the sponge cake in half horizontally to create two thin layers. Briefly dip each sponge layer into the coffee soak and arrange the first layer in the bottom of your serving dish. Spread half of the cream filling over the sponge layer. Place the second soaked sponge layer on top, followed by the remaining cream filling. Smooth the top with a spatula or the back of a spoon.

5. **Chill and Serve:** Dust the top of the tiramisu with cocoa powder and vegan chocolate shavings if desired. Refrigerate for at least 4 hours, or overnight, to set. Serve chilled, cut into squares or slices.

Vegan Key Lime Pie

 8 servings 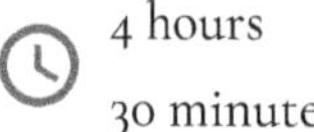 4 hours 30 minutes

INGREDIENTS

For the Crust:
- 1 1/2 cups graham cracker crumbs (ensure vegan)
- 1/3 cup coconut oil, melted
- 1/4 cup granulated sugar

For the Filling:
- 1 cup raw cashews, soaked for 4 hours or overnight, then drained
- 1/2 cup canned coconut milk, well shaken
- 1/2 cup key lime juice (or regular lime juice if key limes are unavailable)
- 1/2 cup maple syrup or agave nectar
- Zest of 2 key limes (or 1 regular lime)
- 1/4 cup coconut oil, melted

For the Coconut Whipped Cream:
- 1 can (14 oz) full-fat coconut milk, chilled overnight
- 2 tablespoons powdered sugar
- 1/2 teaspoon vanilla extract

DIRECTIONS

1. **Prepare the Crust:** Preheat your oven to 350°F (175°C). Mix the graham cracker crumbs, melted coconut oil, and granulated sugar in a bowl until well combined. Press the mixture firmly into the bottom and up the sides of a 9-inch pie dish. Bake for 10 minutes, then remove from the oven and let it cool completely.

2. **Make the Filling:** In a high-speed blender, combine the soaked and drained cashews, coconut milk, key lime juice, maple syrup, lime zest, and melted coconut oil. Blend until the mixture is completely smooth and creamy. Pour the filling into the cooled crust, smoothing the top with a spatula.

3. **Chill the Pie:** Refrigerate the pie for at least 4 hours, or until the filling is firm and set.

4. **Prepare the Coconut Whipped Cream:** Open the chilled can of coconut milk and scoop out the solid cream into a chilled mixing bowl, leaving the liquid behind. Add the powdered sugar and vanilla extract to the bowl. Beat with an electric mixer on high speed until stiff peaks form.

5. **Serve:** Top the chilled pie with coconut whipped cream and garnish with additional lime zest or thin lime slices. Slice and serve the pie chilled.

Vegan Banana Cream Pie

☆☆☆☆☆

🍴 8 servings 🕐 4 hours 30 minutes

INGREDIENTS

For the Crust:
- 1 1/2 cups graham cracker crumbs (ensure vegan)
- 1/3 cup coconut oil, melted
- 1/4 cup granulated sugar

For the Filling:
- 2 1/2 cups canned coconut milk
- 2/3 cup granulated sugar
- 1/3 cup cornstarch
- 1/4 teaspoon salt
- 1 teaspoon vanilla extract
- 2 tablespoons vegan butter
- 3 ripe bananas, sliced

For the Topping:
- 1 can (14 oz) full-fat coconut milk, chilled overnight
- 2 tablespoons powdered sugar
- 1/2 teaspoon vanilla extract

DIRECTIONS

1. **Prepare the Crust:** In a mixing bowl, combine the graham cracker crumbs, melted coconut oil, and sugar until well mixed. Press the mixture firmly into the bottom and up the sides of a 9-inch pie dish. Refrigerate the crust for about 30 minutes to set, or bake at 350°F (175°C) for 10 minutes for a firmer crust. Allow to cool completely.

2. **Make the Filling:** In a saucepan, whisk together the coconut milk, sugar, cornstarch, and salt. Cook over medium heat, whisking constantly, until the mixture thickens and bubbles, about 5-7 minutes. Remove from heat and stir in the vanilla extract and vegan butter until the butter is melted and the mixture is smooth. Arrange a layer of sliced bananas on the bottom of the crust. Pour the filling over the bananas, smoothing the top with a spatula. Chill in the refrigerator until set, about 3-4 hours.

3. **Prepare the Topping:** Open the chilled can of coconut milk and scoop out the solid cream into a chilled mixing bowl, leaving the liquid behind. Add the powdered sugar and vanilla extract. Beat with an electric mixer on high speed until stiff peaks form.

4. **Assemble and Serve:** Once the filling is set, spread the coconut whipped cream evenly over the top. Garnish with additional banana slices or vegan graham cracker crumbs if desired. Keep the pie chilled until ready to serve.

Vegan Pear and Almond Tart

 8 servings    2 hours

INGREDIENTS

For the Crust:

- 1 1/4 cups all-purpose flour (use gluten-free if needed)
- 1/4 cup almond flour
- 1/4 cup powdered sugar
- 1/2 cup vegan butter, cold and cubed
- 2-3 tablespoons ice water

For the Filling:

- 1/2 cup almond flour
- 1/4 cup granulated sugar
- 1/4 cup vegan butter, softened
- 1 teaspoon vanilla extract
- 2 tablespoons almond milk

For the Pear Topping:

- 3-4 ripe pears, peeled, cored, and sliced
- 2 tablespoons apricot jam (for glazing)
- 1/4 cup sliced almonds (for garnish)

DIRECTIONS

1. **Prepare the Crust:** In a food processor, combine the all-purpose flour, almond flour, and powdered sugar. Pulse to mix. Add the cold vegan butter and pulse until the mixture resembles coarse crumbs. Gradually add ice water and pulse until the dough starts to come together. Form the dough into a disc, wrap in plastic wrap, and chill in the refrigerator for at least 1 hour.

2. **Make the Almond Filling:** In a bowl, beat together the almond flour, granulated sugar, softened vegan butter, vanilla extract, and almond milk until smooth and creamy. Set aside.

3. **Assemble the Tart:** Preheat your oven to 350°F (175°C). Roll out the chilled dough on a lightly floured surface into a circle to fit a 9-inch tart pan with a removable bottom. Press the dough into the pan and trim any excess. Spread the almond filling evenly over the crust. Arrange the pear slices on top of the filling in a circular pattern, slightly overlapping.

4. **Bake:** Bake for 40-45 minutes, or until the crust is golden and the filling is set.

5. **Glaze and Garnish:** Heat the apricot jam in a small saucepan over low heat or in the microwave until runny. Brush the jam over the warm pears to glaze. Sprinkle the sliced almonds around the edge of the tart for garnish.

6. **Serve:** Let the tart cool in the pan on a wire rack. Once cooled, remove the tart from the pan, slice, and serve.

Vegan Gingerbread Cookies

 24 cookies 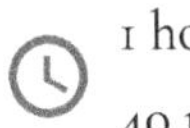 1 hours 40 minutes

INGREDIENTS

- 2 1/4 cups all-purpose flour (use gluten-free flour blend if needed)
- 1 teaspoon baking soda
- 1/4 teaspoon salt
- 2 teaspoons ground ginger
- 1 teaspoon ground cinnamon
- 1/2 teaspoon ground cloves
- 1/4 teaspoon ground nutmeg
- 1/2 cup vegan butter, softened
- 1/2 cup brown sugar, packed
- 1/4 cup molasses
- 1 flax egg (1 tablespoon ground flaxseed mixed with 3 tablespoons water, let sit for 15 minutes)
- 1 teaspoon vanilla extract

For decoration (optional):
- Vegan royal icing
- Sprinkles or edible decorations

DIRECTIONS

1. **Prepare the Dry Ingredients:** In a large bowl, whisk together the flour, baking soda, salt, ginger, cinnamon, cloves, and nutmeg. Set aside.
2. **Cream Butter and Sugar:** In another large bowl, use an electric mixer to cream the vegan butter and brown sugar together until light and fluffy. Add the molasses, flax egg, and vanilla extract, and beat until well combined.
3. **Combine Wet and Dry Ingredients:** Gradually add the dry ingredients to the wet ingredients, mixing until a dough forms. If the dough is too sticky, you can add a little more flour, but be careful not to add too much, as it will dry out the cookies.
4. **Chill the Dough:** Divide the dough in half, wrap in plastic wrap, and chill in the refrigerator for at least 1 hour, or overnight. This step is crucial for the dough to be firm enough to roll out.
5. **Preheat Oven and Prepare Baking Sheets:** Preheat your oven to 350°F (175°C). Line two baking sheets with parchment paper.
6. **Roll Out the Dough:** On a lightly floured surface, roll out one portion of the dough to about 1/4 inch thickness. Use gingerbread cookie cutters to cut out shapes and carefully transfer them to the prepared baking sheets.
7. **Bake:** Bake for 8-10 minutes, or until the edges are just starting to darken. The cookies will firm up as they cool.
8. **Decorate:** Allow the cookies to cool completely on a wire rack before decorating with vegan royal icing and any other edible decorations you like.

Coconut and Lime Vegan Rice Pudding

🍴 4 servings 🕐 35 minutes

INGREDIENTS

- 1 cup Arborio rice or short-grain rice
- 1 can (14 oz) full-fat coconut milk
- 2 cups almond milk (or any plant-based milk)
- 1/3 cup granulated sugar
- Zest of 1 lime
- Juice of 1 lime
- 1 teaspoon vanilla extract
- Pinch of salt
- Toasted coconut flakes, for garnish
- Lime zest, for garnish

DIRECTIONS

1. **Cook the Rice:** In a large saucepan, combine the Arborio rice, coconut milk, almond milk, and a pinch of salt. Bring to a boil over medium heat, then reduce the heat to low and simmer, stirring frequently, until the rice is tender and the mixture has thickened, about 20-25 minutes.
2. **Add Flavor:** Once the rice is cooked, stir in the granulated sugar, lime zest, lime juice, and vanilla extract. Continue to cook for another 5 minutes, stirring occasionally. Taste and adjust sweetness if necessary.
3. **Cool:** Remove the saucepan from the heat and let the rice pudding cool slightly. It will thicken further as it cools.
4. **Serve:** Spoon the rice pudding into serving dishes. Garnish with toasted coconut flakes and additional lime zest. Serve warm or chill in the refrigerator for a cold dessert.
5. **Optional Serving Suggestions:** For an extra touch of sweetness, drizzle a little maple syrup or agave nectar over the top before serving. Add a sprinkle of cinnamon or cardamom for a hint of spice.

Vegan Chocolate Avocado Truffles

 16 truffles  1 hours 50 minutes

INGREDIENTS

- 2 ripe avocados, peeled and pitted
- 1/2 cup cocoa powder, plus extra for rolling
- 1/2 cup dark chocolate chips (vegan)
- 3-4 tablespoons maple syrup, adjust to taste
- 1 teaspoon vanilla extract
- A pinch of salt

DIRECTIONS

1. **Melt the Chocolate:** Gently melt the dark chocolate chips in a microwave-safe bowl in 30-second intervals, stirring between each, until smooth. Alternatively, use a double boiler on the stove.
2. **Blend the Ingredients:** In a food processor, blend the avocados until smooth. Add the melted chocolate, cocoa powder, maple syrup, vanilla extract, and a pinch of salt. Blend again until the mixture is completely smooth and well combined.
3. **Chill the Mixture:** Transfer the truffle mixture to a bowl and refrigerate for at least 1 hour, or until the mixture is firm enough to handle.
4. **Form the Truffles:** Once chilled, use a spoon or melon baller to scoop out portions of the mixture. Roll each portion into a ball between your palms. If the mixture sticks to your hands, lightly dust them with cocoa powder.
5. **Coat the Truffles:** Roll each truffle in additional cocoa powder, shaking off the excess. For variation, you can also roll truffles in chopped nuts, shredded coconut, or vegan sprinkles.
6. **Chill Again:** Place the finished truffles on a parchment-lined plate or tray. Chill in the refrigerator for another 30 minutes to set.
7. **Serve:** Serve the truffles chilled. They can be stored in an airtight container in the refrigerator for up to a week.

Vegan Orange and Almond Cake

 8 servings 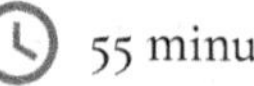 55 minutes

INGREDIENTS

For the Cake:

- 1 1/2 cups all-purpose flour (use gluten-free if needed)
- 1 cup almond flour
- 1 cup granulated sugar
- 1 teaspoon baking powder
- 1/2 teaspoon baking soda
- 1/2 teaspoon salt
- Zest of 2 oranges
- 3/4 cup fresh orange juice (from about 2–3 oranges)
- 1/2 cup almond milk (or any plant-based milk)
- 1/3 cup vegetable oil
- 2 teaspoons apple cider vinegar
- 1 teaspoon vanilla extract

For the Orange Glaze:

- 1 cup powdered sugar
- 2–3 tablespoons fresh orange juice
- 1/2 teaspoon orange zest (for garnish)
- Sliced almonds (for garnish)

DIRECTIONS

1. **Prepare the Cake:** Preheat your oven to 350°F (175°C). Grease and flour an 8-inch round cake pan, or line it with parchment paper. In a large bowl, whisk together the all-purpose flour, almond flour, granulated sugar, baking powder, baking soda, salt, and orange zest. In another bowl, mix together the orange juice, almond milk, vegetable oil, apple cider vinegar, and vanilla extract. Add the wet ingredients to the dry ingredients and stir until just combined, being careful not to overmix.

2. **Bake:** Pour the batter into the prepared cake pan. Bake for 35-40 minutes, or until a toothpick inserted into the center comes out clean. Let the cake cool in the pan for 10 minutes, then transfer it to a wire rack to cool completely.

3. **Prepare the Orange Glaze:** In a small bowl, whisk together the powdered sugar and enough orange juice to achieve a pourable consistency.

4. **Assemble and Serve:** Once the cake has cooled, drizzle the orange glaze over the top. Garnish with orange zest and sliced almonds. Allow the glaze to set before slicing and serving.

Vegan Peanut Butter and Jelly Cupcakes

🍴 12 cupcakes   🕐 50 minutes

INGREDIENTS

For the Cupcakes:

- 1 3/4 cups all-purpose flour (use gluten-free if needed)
- 1 cup granulated sugar
- 1 teaspoon baking powder
- 1/2 teaspoon baking soda
- 1/2 teaspoon salt
- 3/4 cup almond milk (or any plant-based milk)
- 1/2 cup creamy peanut butter
- 1/3 cup vegetable oil
- 1 tablespoon apple cider vinegar
- 1 teaspoon vanilla extract

For the Filling:

- 1/2 cup your favorite jelly or jam

For the Peanut Butter Frosting:

- 1/2 cup vegan butter, softened
- 1 cup creamy peanut butter
- 2 cups powdered sugar, sifted
- 2-3 tablespoons almond milk (or any plant-based milk)
- 1 teaspoon vanilla extract

DIRECTIONS

1. **Prepare the Cupcakes:** Preheat your oven to 350°F (175°C). Line a muffin tin with cupcake liners. In a large bowl, whisk together the flour, sugar, baking powder, baking soda, and salt. In another bowl, mix the almond milk, peanut butter, vegetable oil, apple cider vinegar, and vanilla extract until smooth. Add the wet ingredients to the dry ingredients and stir until just combined. Do not overmix.

2. **Bake:** Fill each cupcake liner about 2/3 full with the batter. Bake for 18-20 minutes, or until a toothpick inserted into the center comes out clean. Allow the cupcakes to cool in the pan for 5 minutes, then transfer them to a wire rack to cool completely.

3. **Fill the Cupcakes:** Once the cupcakes are cool, use a knife or a cupcake corer to remove a small piece from the center of each cupcake. Fill the hole with a spoonful of jelly or jam.

4. **Make the Peanut Butter Frosting:** In a large bowl, beat together the vegan butter and peanut butter until smooth. Gradually add the powdered sugar, beating until fluffy. Mix in the almond milk and vanilla extract until the frosting reaches a spreadable consistency.

5. **Decorate:** Frost each cupcake with the peanut butter frosting. If desired, you can use a piping bag and tip for a more decorative look.

6. **Serve:** Enjoy the cupcakes as they are, or garnish with a dollop of jelly, a sprinkle of crushed peanuts, or vegan chocolate chips.

Vegan Mango and Passion Fruit Sorbet

 4 servings

4 hours 15 minutes

INGREDIENTS

- 2 ripe mangoes, peeled and chopped
- Pulp of 4 passion fruits
- 1/2 cup granulated sugar (adjust based on sweetness of the fruit)
- 1/2 cup water
- Juice of 1 lime

DIRECTIONS

1. **Prepare the Simple Syrup:** In a small saucepan, combine the sugar and water. Bring to a boil over medium heat, stirring until the sugar has dissolved. Remove from heat and allow it to cool to room temperature.
2. **Blend the Fruits:** In a blender, combine the chopped mangoes, passion fruit pulp, and lime juice. Blend until the mixture is smooth.
3. **Combine with Simple Syrup:** Strain the fruit mixture through a fine mesh sieve to remove any seeds or fibers, pressing down to extract as much liquid as possible. Mix the strained fruit mixture with the cooled simple syrup. Stir well to combine.
4. **Chill the Mixture:** Cover and refrigerate the sorbet mixture for at least 2 hours, until completely chilled.
5. **Churn the Sorbet:** Pour the chilled mixture into an ice cream maker and churn according to the manufacturer's instructions, usually about 20-25 minutes, until it reaches a soft-serve consistency.
6. **Freeze to Set:** Transfer the churned sorbet to a freezer-safe container. Cover and freeze until firm, usually about 2-3 hours, depending on your freezer.
7. **Serve:** Let the sorbet sit at room temperature for a few minutes to soften slightly before scooping. Serve in bowls or cones, garnished with fresh mint leaves or additional passion fruit pulp if desired.

Vegan Caramel Apples

 6-8 caramel apples    2-3 hours

INGREDIENTS

- 6-8 medium apples, washed and thoroughly dried
- 1 cup granulated sugar
- 1/2 cup light corn syrup
- 1/4 cup water
- 1/2 cup coconut cream (the thick part from the top of a can of full-fat coconut milk)
- 2 tablespoons vegan butter
- 1 teaspoon vanilla extract
- Pinch of salt

For Dipping and Topping:
- Chopped nuts (like pecans or almonds)
- Vegan chocolate chips
- Shredded coconut

Other:
- Popsicle sticks or skewers

DIRECTIONS

1. **Prepare the Apples:** Insert a popsicle stick or skewer firmly into the top of each apple. Line a baking sheet with parchment paper and grease it lightly with vegan butter or coconut oil.
2. **Make the Vegan Caramel:** In a medium, heavy-bottomed saucepan, combine the sugar, corn syrup, and water. Cook over medium heat, stirring occasionally, until the sugar has dissolved. Increase the heat to bring the mixture to a boil. Do not stir once the mixture is boiling. Continue to cook until it reaches 250°F (120°C) on a candy thermometer. Carefully stir in the coconut cream, vegan butter, vanilla extract, and a pinch of salt. The mixture will bubble up, so be cautious. Continue to cook, stirring constantly, until the caramel reaches 248°F (120°C), suitable for a firm caramel. Remove from heat and let the caramel cool slightly until it thickens a bit but is still dip-able.
3. **Dip the Apples:** Dip each apple into the caramel, tilting the pot if needed and turning the apple to coat it evenly. Allow the excess caramel to drip off. If desired, roll the dipped apples in chopped nuts, vegan chocolate chips, or shredded coconut for extra texture and flavor. Place the coated apples on the prepared baking sheet to set.
4. **Let the Caramel Set:** Allow the caramel apples to cool and set at room temperature. If in a hurry, you can refrigerate them for a faster setting, but they're best enjoyed at room temperature for easier eating.
5. **Serve and Enjoy:** Once the caramel is set, the vegan caramel apples are ready to be enjoyed. Serve them the same day for the best texture and flavor.